Develo  rs
terly

42

MAKING ORGANIZATIO

Driving Sustainability

Catalyzing your leadership practice

Publisher's note

Every effort has been made to ensure information contained in this publication is accurate at the time of going to press. Neither the publishers nor any of the contributors can accept responsibility for any errors or omissions, however caused, nor for any loss or damage occasioned to any person acting, or refraining from action, as a result of the material in this publication.

Users and readers of this publication may copy portions of the material for personal use, internal reports, or reports to clients provided that such articles (or portions of articles) are attributed to this publication by name, the individual contributor of the portion uses and publisher.

IEDP Ideas for Leaders Ltd
42 Moray Place, Edinburgh, EH3 6BT
www.ideasforleaders.com

in association with the Center for the Future of Organization at the
Drucker School of Management
www.futureorg.org

Publishers: Roland Deiser and Roddy Millar
Editor-in-Chief: Roddy Millar
Senior Editor: Roland Deiser
Associate Editors: Saar Ben-Attar (Africa), Suzie Lewis (Europe)
Conrado Schlochauer (LatAm), Ravi Shankar (SE Asia)
Art Direction: Nick Mortimer – nickmortimer.co.uk

 WORLD LAND TRUST™ Printed by Pureprint, a Carbon Neutral® Company, on an FSC certified paper from responsible sources. The paper is Carbon Balanced with the World Land Trust, an international conservation charity who offset carbon emissions through the purchase of high conservation land value.

ISBN 978-1-91-552922-0 (Paperback)
ISBN 978-1-91-552923-7 (e-Pub)
ISSN 2044-2203 (Developing Leaders Quarterly)

www.developingleadersquarterly.com

Contents

Sustainability is today both something we passionately strive for and also something we, all too often, treat with a glib disregard. In this issue **Henry Mintzberg (page 8)**, one of the greatest management thinkers of the last half-century, reflects with Roland Deiser on his journey from critiquing management education to his concerns for bigger macro issues of society and our dangerous disregard and the diminution of influence of what he terms 'the plural sector'.

I would like to think that all readers of DLQ do not doubt the existential dangers of climate change; the Anthropocene era has clearly wrought changes we never considered or understood at the outset of our great shifts from being largely nomadic to largely static inhabitors of our territories, and with that the shift to pastoral and increasingly intensive agrarian production. The last few moments of this human era, since the industrial revolution transformed lives to extraordinary prosperity and comfort, have also been the most destructive to the major natural systems that control our environment. The speed of change in geological terms has been astounding, and our opportunity to reverse our trajectory is equally shocking in its fleetingness.

My definition of leadership is *'to create the conditions for others to do their best work, in pursuit of a common objective'*. On this basis the leader's role is clear: to shape and enable environments so that the 'magic of collaborative human endeavour' can achieve remarkable outcomes. The tricky part lies in the final clause of the above definition, 'the pursuit of a common objective'. Is the organization's objective to maximise profits or, as **Andrea Barrack, Walid Hejazi** and **Susan McGeachie** suggest in their important article (**page 30**) on ESG myths, does the impact of double materiality also need to be factored into the organizational equation?

When we make the issue personal, as **Rolf Pfeiffer** recalls in a story from a WEF event in his article (**page 145**), senior executives quickly find their human sides and see issues not in the black and red of short-term balance sheets, but the blue and green of planetary balance.

As **Melea Press** points out (**page 85**), doing sustainability in organizations too often quickly falls into an additional layer of measurements and report-writing, that deadens the energy to engage in sustainable practice, and makes it too expensive for many SMEs.

Presuming that the strategic will of the common objective is achieved, and that the operational hurdles are embraced, the major barrier to sustainable progress all-too-often remains culture. Without leaders 'creating the conditions' for people to make choices that are longer-term and focused on the double-bottom line of society as well as profit, our journey to healthier organizations will be slow. **Natalie Beinisch** and **Deborah Edward's** article (**page 66**) on their work to enabling this kind of progress in Nigeria is refreshing and uplifting, and **Prof Rosina Watson** (**page 46**) brings her practice-formed views further highlighting the effort required.

Building on the theme of effort, **Andrew Dyckhoff** writes (**page 166**) on the often overlooked importance of organizational energy in making things happen. The returning theme of 'creating the conditions' for that, and magic will happen.

In other pieces **Julian Roberts** explores (**page 150**) how to achieve team resilience in the midst of complexity and change. And **Marilyn Mehlmann** shares (**page 186**) some wonderful insights and wisdom from the Essenes at the time of Christ, based on their ancient principles, underscoring that very little of what enables good organizational design and culture is truly new.

And, as usual, we highlight some insights from our *Ideas for Leaders* library and share some relevant book reviews.

As ever, plenty to stimulate your thinking and catalyze your leadership practice.

Roddy Millar | Editor-in-Chief

If you have any stories you would like to share with us for potential pieces in the magazine or for discussion on the DLQ website, please let me know at **editor@dl-q.com**.

Thinking imprinted.

The first step on any leadership development process is to create space and condition for reflection on your leadership practice.

Multiple studies have concluded that we absorb and digest information better when we read off the printed page. Reading is focused, uninterrupted and, with the chance to note down our own thoughts in the margins, print allows us to actively engage with the subject.

To embed the change, Developing Leaders Quarterly is best in print.

Developing Leaders Quarterly print edition is ideally formatted to slip into your pocket, bag or briefcase to read when you find you have a few minutes to spare before a business guest arrives, while commuting, at the airport...

SUBSCRIBE AT DEVELOPINGLEADERSQUARTERLY.COM/SUBSCRIBE

Roland Deiser in Conversation
with Henry Mintzberg

Rebalancing Society

DLQ's co-publisher, Roland Deiser, caught up with Henry Mintzberg for this issue. Mintzberg, now in his 80s, is one of the great shapers of management thinking over the last half-century, with his acclaimed books on the weaknesses of management education , the fallacies of strategic planning, the real life of managers, and more. In the last decade he has turned his attention to more macro issues.

Roland Deiser

Henry, you've always been a maverick in that community of business scholars – I think about *The Rise and Fall of Strategic Planning*, or *Managers, not MBAs*. But over the last few years you have been passionately writing about 'rebalancing society'. How did you get there? What made that passion come true?

I've always been very aware of the dysfunctions of how we teach management - that we take inexperienced people, put them through two years in an MBA program, and then imagine that they're capable of managing organizations.

Henry Mintzberg

I wrote about management and all that, but I always had that predisposition to think about those broader issues. As I say in the book, *Rebalancing Society,* I visited Prague in 1991. And the thing that struck me, particularly in the United States, that they kept talking about the triumph of capitalism - and it didn't look to me like that at all. I've always been suspicious of this idea that this was a battle between communism and capitalism - and that capitalism won. It seemed to me that communism largely collapsed under its own dead-weight. We didn't recognize that it wasn't capitalism that triumphed, but some kind of balance in society that triumphed back then.

This thing about 'capitalism triumphed' struck me and I started to keep notes like I do. And I have these boxes that are about this big, and I started throwing notes into those boxes. And when two boxes were full of notes and articles and things that I found, I opened them up and wrote an initial pamphlet, and then turned that into the book.

RD So, you shifted your perspective - from the company or the business level to the political level, right? It's not about business schools or strategy. It's really about the large-scale challenges we face on the planet and in societies.

HM Yes. But I've always been very aware of the dysfunctions of how we teach management - that we take inexperienced people, put them through two years in an MBA program, and then imagine that they're capable of managing organizations.

RD We're having this conversation because this issue of Developing Leaders Quarterly is on Driving Sustainability. And your rebalancing society approach is sustainability on a really large, global scale. You are talking about rebuilding society.

HM Yes. And sustainability is threatened. We've got three superpowers that are back to the Cold War, in a way. One of them – China - is out of balance on the side of the public sector, one is out of balance on the side of the private sector – that's America, and one is out of bounds on the side of the plural sector, namely Russia, with its nationalism. And this is dangerous. We're just watching and doing nothing about what could be disastrous.

RD Before we go into this, it may help to explain a little bit what the plural sector is, how you think about that. Because not everybody might have read your work on this.

HM You can say it's my label for civil society, or what people call the not-for-profit sector, or the community sector. It's basically organizations and associations that are largely community-based. Their key defining character is that they are owned neither by governments, nor by investors. We've got huge numbers of not-for-profit or community organizations, associations, civil society - whatever you want to call them. And yet, we don't recognize the sector as a sector.

In fact, the sector suffers from a plethora of names. I think you need a label that is on one level with public and private. So, I came up with Plural, as the third one, next to Public and Private. It's got a huge variety of organizations; we need to recognize that. And once we do, maybe we can start to recognize that balance must be across all three sectors. Tocqueville wrote in the 1830s about associations being the key to American democracy. And he meant literally what I'm calling the plural sector.

> *Tocqueville wrote in the 1830s about associations being the key to American democracy. And he meant literally what I'm calling the plural sector.*

RD You also talk about movements, social movements. And you mention in your book that there are also movements like the Nazis or, maybe more contemporary, the Proud Boys or the mob that went for the Capitol on January 6.

HM And they're also the plural sector, yes. It's not wonderful. But there are enough people organizing in that sector to overwhelm them if they got their collective act together. If I meet Greenpeace, or Greta in Stockholm

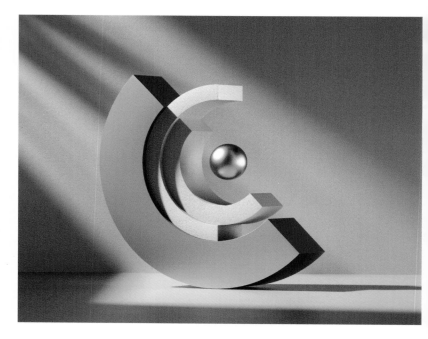

- the first thing I say to them is if you're worried about climate change, then put your energy into rebalancing society, because we will get nowhere until we rebalance our societies.

Every major trend in society, it seems to me, is in the direction of things getting worse, not better. The trends in the plural sector are massive, disorganized, and very significant, but they are nowhere compared to the over-all trends. Look at economic globalization, for example. John Kenneth Galbraith wrote a book about countervail-

If I meet Greenpeace, or Greta in Stockholm - the first thing I say to them is if you're worried about climate change, then put your energy into rebalancing society, because we will get nowhere until we rebalance our societies

ing powers; that when the large American corporations built up, the unions built up as a countervailing force. There is no countervailing force to economic globalization now, certainly not the United Nations, certainly not any particular nation.

Climate change is the best example, or take income disparities. We talk about it incessantly. And it doesn't change. It gets worse. It gets worse, and nobody addresses the major issues. Whether it's climate change, or populism, or the decline of democracy, or income disparities - whatever it is, they're all moving in the wrong direction. I'm stunned at how stupid we are, that we don't recognize this and stand up to it. That's why I wrote *Rebalancing Society*. It enables us to move forward in a consolidated way. Have you seen the website Rebalancingsociety.org? That's the next step. A call to action, what to do.

RD I think you're super strong in diagnostics, Henry. And most people will subscribe to virtually everything you say here. The question is, what is the therapy? What I hear you saying, at the end of your book, is that the solution is the "power of two", you and me. We have to stand up, we've got to be responsible and do our part. Is there more to that? Or is that it? What about governance structures on a global scale?

HM Yeah, I'm working on something. I've blogged about it. About the D24. The Economist ranks countries on a democratic index every year. Full democracies, flawed democracies, hybrid regimes and autocracies. 24 countries are full democracies, out of 180, or so. They're mostly small, Norway is first, the Scandinavian countries are in the top five, New Zealand and Germany's there, Britain's there, Canada's there. Japan is the largest of the 24 - and it's only the 11th largest country in the world by population. So, the 10 largest countries of the world are not there. We have a G7, and a G20 - all of them big, powerful countries. Maybe we need a D24. The 24 democratic countries that can stand as a counter to these big aggressive, largely bullying countries - and particularly stand up to the three superpowers. So, I published a piece called *Superpower Corrupts*, about the superpowers and the D24.

Who consolidated that? Nobody consolidated that. Everybody consolidated that. Same thing with Eastern Europe. It wasn't just Lech Walesa, in Poland, it wasn't just people knocking down the wall in Berlin, it was everything together. The time was right, and people just did it.

On the website, I talk about three stages of change. Stage one is some commitment to a belief system - the declaration of interdependence that people sign. Stage two are local actions, community actions. And stage three is consolidation. And I thought, how do you consolidate? How do you get all the NGOs that are worried about climate change to consolidate around rebalancing society? I figured that the most important thing I could do at this point is to study social movements that have been successful. Eastern Europe in 1989, the American Civil Rights Movement, the quiet revolution in Quebec, etc.

The most interesting one to me is the Reformation. Here's this obscure monk.

He writes these theses down on a sheet of paper and he puts it up against the door of an obscure church. I don't know what followed in detail, but his students saw it, took it down and used the social media of the time – namely the printing press - to circulate 300,000 copies, leading to the Reformation, to Protestantism, and so on. Who consolidated that? Nobody consolidated that. Everybody consolidated that. Same thing with Eastern Europe. It wasn't just Lech Walesa, in Poland, it wasn't just people knocking down the wall in Berlin, it was everything together. The time was right, and people just did it.

RD But there was also a context that eventually led to that. People just had enough with all the corruption that went on in the Catholic Church, where you could pay off your sins. Arab Spring is another good example. But on the other hand, we can see the dark force beat back. We've got now in Egypt not such a great regime. We've got Syria, where people rose up - to what result?

HM Yeah, well, Quebec changed dramatically. Quebec was the most locked-in Catholic place you can imagine, and it's probably the most progressive place in North America today - the first one to accept gay marriage, and so on. Christianity didn't go away, despite the Reformation. It superseded the Catholic Church. The Civil Rights

Movement was largely successful – which doesn't mean it's finished. And then, yes, you have the Arab Spring, that reverted right back, all kinds of countries reverting back. You have to go by what works.

RD Well, Henry, we're talking here very large scale, on a societal level. What about we go down just a bit, to the

The pressure of the stock market is more, more, more – but not more quality, more quantity.

private sector, as you call it. We know how much green-washing is happening. But there are also top executives who have the right values - who really want to make a difference. How do you see these serious sustainability efforts and strategies in large companies?

HM I'm not one for simple solutions. But here's one simple solution: get them the hell off the stock market! The stock market is utterly dysfunctional. Absolutely. When Apple passed a trillion dollars in stock value for the first time, that was the beginning for the stock market to think - what are you doing tomorrow? We get people building up great companies, and once they go public, the pressure of the stock market is more, more, more – but not more quality, more quantity. Tell me if you think I'm wrong, but the secret to the brilliance of the German economy, despite recent things - I would attribute that to quality, not quantity.

RD Well, what you have in Germany is, of course, the so-called Mittelstand. These SMEs with up to maybe 10-15,000 people, 3 to 5 billion revenue, still owned by families who are not going on the stock market. They have other issues, typical for family-owned businesses, like family dynamics, succession, and all that kind of stuff. But it's a different kind of pressure.

HM Exactly. And in Scandinavia, particularly in Denmark, most of the companies are set up as trusts. So, the voting shares are not controlled by the stock market. The same thing with Tata in India. They have publicly listed shares, but they're not beholden to kid analysts who tell them what to do.

RD Exactly. This also relates to our work on business ecosystem engagement. One thing that keeps companies from embracing the profitability of their larger ecosystem is the focus on shareholder value that focuses them on maximizing their own profits.

HM Yeah. And the other thing is that it brings down the management. Entrepreneurs are committed to their ideas. But as they reach a certain size, professional management is taking over who doesn't have those ideas. So they'd find other ways to grow, manipulate and play games and charge for things that they shouldn't be charging for, nickel and diming their customers, and so on and so forth.

RD Ok, so it's shareholder value, public listing, the quarterly pressure, and more that works against good intentions. But let's talk about the other side, too, about

You know who is my target market? It's people without mortgages. People who don't have mortgages are under 30 and over 70. Because between 30 and 70, the attitude is 'yes, that's a good idea, somebody should do something about that – but I'm busy.' Under 30-people are serious, over 70-people are serious

things that inspire. One of the authors of this DLQ issue is Natalie Beinisch, the wife of a Shell executive who is based in Lagos, Nigeria. Instead of settling into a typical life of an expat-wife, she started a circular economy initiative connecting startups, government agencies, companies, and what not, so she can foster sustainability in one of the toughest places on the planet. It's really a very inspiring story. So, you want to get these things more visibility? Is that what you're up to?

HM Am I wishing these things more visibility? Yes! I'm writing to raise consciousness about what I see as the prime cause of what's bringing us down. Whether it's income disparities, the fall of democracy, or climate change, or whatever it is. That's where I'm devoting my attention.

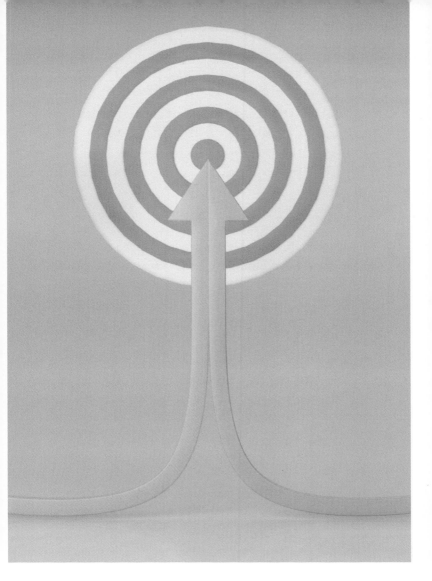

I am trying to reach people who care, I don't care if they're businesspeople, or government, people, or anything else, as long as they care. And they can figure out what they can do in their own institutions.

RD So, what are your hopes? Gaining more signatures on the declaration? Is there a way to inspire or engage also the business community? Is there any relationship you can create with governments or governance bodies?

HM Well, I think this kind of change, like the Reformation, starts on the ground, it doesn't start with institutions. Institutions join when there's enough of a movement. So, I am trying to reach people who care, I don't care if they're businesspeople, or government, people, or anything else, as long as they care. And they can figure out what they can do in their own institutions. You know who is my target market? It's people without mortgages. People who don't have mortgages are under 30 and over 70. Because between 30 and 70, the attitude is 'yes, that's a good idea, somebody should do something about that - but I'm busy.' Under 30-people are serious, over 70-people are serious.

RD That sounds like a great coalition. I'm super impressed by your passion, Henry. Best of luck. Let's hope in the interest of all of us that the awareness of the plural sector's importance grows and your ideas get as much success as possible.

The full interview recording is available to our subscribers on the DLQ website. Here we publish edited highlights from the conversation.

Henry Mintzberg *is the Cleghorn Professor of Management Studies at McGill University. He is the author of over 180 articles and 21 books, among them* Managers, Not MBAs; Simply Managing; Bedtime stories for managers, Understanding Organizations *– and most recently* Rebalancing society *with its website* **www.rebalancingsociety.org**. *He twice received the McKinsey Award for best articles in The Harvard Business Review. More at* **www.mintzberg.org**

Roland Deiser *is a Senior Drucker Fellow and Founding Chairman of the Center for the Future of Organization at the Drucker School of Management at Claremont Graduate University (***www.futureorg.org***). He is the author of several books, articles, and research reports and also serves as the Co-Publisher and Senior Editor of Developing Leaders Quarterly.*

Andrea Barrack,
Walid Hejazi and
Susan McGeachie

Integrating ESG in an Organization's DNA

E SG, or Environment, Social and Governance is emerging as one of the most critical management imperatives facing leaders across organizations. It is no longer a viable option for these issues to be relegated to the fringe of corporate priorities, rather it has become necessary that organizations embed these issues in corporate strategy and risk management practices. Increasingly, organizations are required to report their ESG performance so that both internal and external stakeholders can make informed decisions about their association with them. Organizations must therefore achieve and report tangible and meaningful progress towards achieving strong ESG outcomes.

It is no longer a viable option for these issues to be relegated to the fringe of corporate priorities, rather it has become necessary that organizations embed these issues in corporate strategy and risk management practices

As data standards for reporting ESG performance improve and better alignment on ESG reporting frameworks emerges, organizations will increasingly be required to report, and be benchmarked against, industry peers. This growing scrutiny and, increasingly, legal disclosure requirements, require attention from the most senior leadership within organizations.

This article will cover three themes. First, we highlight four common myths associated with ESG, which if not understood can lead to poor ESG outcomes. We demonstrate that those who fully understand ESG can deploy more effective ESG strategies, which transform such progress into enhanced competitiveness and business opportunities. Second, we review some of the key stakeholders that are disciplining organizations to improve their ESG performance, and how these stakeholders are shaping the ESG landscape. Third, we high-

light that when ESG is approached strategically and fully integrated into organizational cultures, it can be a source of competitive advantage.

1. ESG Myths

Myth 1. *ESG is all about climate.*

ESG includes issues related to climate and environmental sustainability, which covers the E, and is the component of ESG that gets the most attention both by leaders and many stakeholders, including the media. We are all aware of the risks associated with carbon emissions, and the need to achieve net zero by 2050. The catastrophic implications of not achieving this goal have been well documented, and while much work has been done in this respect, there is much more to do. In addition, there are increasingly material "E" topics like biodiversity, deforestation and water, which are gaining traction.

But ESG goes far beyond environmental sustainability alone. It also includes S, or Social. This is a very broad pillar and includes human rights and treatment of employees and customers within organizations and across global supply chains. "S" also incorporates issues of diversity and inclusion, how the organization impacts the communities they serve, including indigenous communities, and many other issues.

And finally, ESG includes the G, or Governance, which incorporates how organizations are managed, risk management, and business ethics. It is often the case that deficiencies in governance processes end up in the news as scandals – such as the Audi emissions scandal, Facebook's privacy violations, and many others too numerous to list.

Those leaders that focus on E alone are only addressing a narrow slice of the full spectrum of ESG issues and are therefore more likely to face challenges from shareholders and other stakeholders, miss interdependencies, and be caught unprepared for increasing ESG disclosure requirements. While E may get most of the attention, there is accelerating focus on the other dimensions of ESG that cannot be ignored.

Myth 2. *ESG is handled by a department in corporate functions.*

It is often viewed that an ESG department, executive or committee will suffice to ensure an organization has appropriate oversight of ESG issues. While specific accountability is helpful, this siloed approach can hinder the organization in making the required progress. Such an approach often results in an ineffective "tick the boxes" approach to ESG.

This is in sharp contrast to an approach in which every decision is made through an ESG lens. As the well-known saying goes, "culture eats strategy for breakfast". For organizations to fully integrate ESG into each of its decisions, that is, into its DNA, it is essential that ESG be part of the culture of the organization. Many organizations have implemented extensive training sessions to ingrain ESG strategies into each of the organization's functional areas – finance, strategy, HR, marketing, operations, innovation and design, and leadership training itself.

When this is done well, there will be no need for a separate office within organizations to oversee ESG because ESG will be ingrained in everything the organization does. However, change takes time and ESG is still nascent in its maturity for most organizations. While the ultimate goal is for full integration of an ESG lens, consistent with the organization's culture, most organizations are still developing the structures and mindset through specialized functions.

Myth 3. *ESG is about the impact a business has on society and the environment.*

A limited view of ESG often held by many is that impact is a one-way street, focused on the impact a business has on society and the environment. The task force on Climate-related Financial Disclosures (TCFD) was amongst the first to highlight the impact of climate change on a company's financial performance, including the future potential price of the carbon it emits, and other societal and technological headwinds that could impact future performance. Insurance companies, for example, are feeling the impact of climate change by paying record claims for flooding and damage related to extreme weather. Consumer packaging companies are experiencing the impact of natural disasters on their supply chains. While extensive wildfire smoke within Canada during the summer of 2023 have resulted in significant disruptions to business, with the expectation of many costly health implications to follow.

The focus on the financial impact of climate change and other ESG factors on an organization became the litmus test for evaluating materiality to such a large

Organizations will increasingly be required to report, and be benchmarked against, industry peers

extent that stakeholders began deprioritizing the organization's impact on society and the environment. To curb the outcomes of such a complete shift, the idea of double materiality emerged, which recognizes both the impact ESG factors have on a business, and the impact a business has on such issues.

Myth 4. *ESG is a form of Woke Capitalism.*
In some jurisdictions, ESG has become politicized, and labelled Woke Capitalism. This development reflects a misunderstanding of what a focus on ESG is meant to achieve. The increasing rigour of reporting on ESG data that is relevant to business strategy and objectives is very different than the accusation that businesses are using their influence to advocate for social and environmental causes. They are two completely different topics. ESG was first coined in 2005 in a United Nations commissioned report by law firm Freshfields Bruckhaus Deringer, which found that "failure to consider all long term investment value drivers, including ESG issues, is a failure of fiduciary duty". ESG analytics were so focused

ESG goes far beyond environmental sustainability alone. It also includes S, or Social and the G, or Governance. Those leaders that focus on E alone are only addressing a narrow slice of the full spectrum of ESG

on the impact to a company's future financial performance that, in 2021, Bloomberg critically observed that '[ESG] ratings don't measure a company's impact on the Earth and society. In fact, they gauge the opposite: the potential impact of the world on the company and its shareholders.' In its consideration of ESG integration, however, the Freshfields report was more prescient, reflecting on how investors' duties and obligations may further evolve over time with shifts in societal expectations, policies, technologies, and the climate.

Ten years later, Mark Carney, then Governor of the Bank of England, suggested this time had arrived in a speech on the impact of climate change on financial stability. Now the UN Special Envoy on Climate Action and Finance, Chair of Brookfield Asset Management and Head of Transition Investing at Brookfield Corporation, Mr. Carney notes that 'companies are recognizing that they are not islands, independent of the social system,

political system, economic system or climatic system. They are connected and take responsibility for those connections and help those to whom they are connected to move forward. With COVID-19, a sense of solidarity has grown and added to a sense of purpose for many companies.'

2. Stakeholders are raising the stakes!

Stakeholders have been defined as "those groups who affect and/or could be affected by an organization's activities, products or services and associated performance." **The list of stakeholders is often much broader than many leaders realize.** While there are stakeholders common to many organizations, the relative importance of these stakeholders will vary depending on the impact the organization can have on them, and the impact they

Paying close attention to all stakeholders is not a political agenda, but rather it makes good business sense

can have on the organization. As such, each organization should develop an appropriate stakeholder engagement strategy to ensure it fully understands the issues of importance to each stakeholder group, be able to manage conflicting interests across stakeholders, and to develop strategies to most effectively deal with those issues.

We now review the most important stakeholders for most organizations.

Financial Markets

Perhaps first on the list of many leaders are financial markets. An increasing number of investors across the spectrum are insisting that the companies they invest in perform well on ESG, with a requirement that the ESG performance be objectively measured and reported.

This trend was cemented by Larry Fink when he wrote in his 2020 letter to CEOs.

"But awareness is rapidly changing, and I believe we are on the edge of a fundamental reshaping of finance. The evidence on climate risk is compelling investors to reassess core assumptions about

modern finance. ... Investors are increasingly reckoning with these questions and recognizing that climate risk is investment risk. ...These questions are driving a profound reassessment of risk and asset values. And because capital markets pull future risk forward, we will see changes in capital allocation more quickly than we see changes to the climate itself. In the near future – and sooner than most anticipate – there will be a significant reallocation of capital. ... As a fiduciary, our responsibility is to help clients navigate this transition. Our investment conviction is that sustainability – and climate-integrated portfolios can provide better risk-adjusted returns to investors."

Estimates now put the level of investable assets committed to companies that have achieved an acceptable level of ESG performance in excess of US$30 trillion and growing. These investors are demanding that ESG performance be verifiable using objective metrics to back up such claims. Younger investors, namely millennials and Generation Zs, are twice as likely to use an ESG lens in making their investment decisions. As these trends increasingly permeate financial markets, the cost of capital for organizations with poor ESG performance will increase, thus impacting their competitiveness and profitability. In contrast, organizations that outperform on ESG will have a lower cost of and priority access to capital.

Employees

ESG performance is also an important issue to employees. Increasingly, companies that do not perform well in terms of ESG have difficulty both attracting and retaining talent. In sharp contrast, those organizations that embrace ESG have a competitive advantage in this regard.

Employees are increasingly leaving organizations that are viewed as poor ESG performers. There are many examples of companies that serve as case studies on the importance of ESG as a recruitment strategy.

One such case study published in in Canada's national business newspaper, *The Globe and Mail*, documents how employees seek employment in firms that are ESG leaders. "Eco-friendly retailer Tentree doesn't have to advertise its carbon-reduction efforts to potential hires. Most applicants are familiar with the Vancouver-based company's values and mission, including the trees it plants with every purchase, and are looking to join the company partly because of it, says founder and chief executive officer Derrick Emsley." And this is just one example among many.

This pattern is confirmed in a survey conducted by PwC, which found that "86 per cent of employees 'prefer to support or work for companies that care about the

Companies that do not perform well in terms of ESG have difficulty both attracting and retaining talent. Employees are increasingly leaving organizations that are viewed as poor ESG performers

same issues they do,' and that 84 per cent are more likely to work for a company that stands up for environmental causes." And the evidence goes further, indicating that workers who are satisfied "work harder, stay longer with their employers, and seek to produce better results for the organization." These trends are expected to accelerate as millennials and Gen Zs make up an increasing share of the labour force.

Disclosing their suppliers would incentivize retailers to ensure working conditions were up to their stated standards

Civil Society

There have been many organizations that have reacted strongly against companies that cause harm along their supply chains. According to the Harvard Business Review, "Companies are under pressure from governments, consumers, NGOs, and other stakeholders to divulge more information about their supply chains, and the reputational cost of failing to meet these demands can be high." Perhaps the most well-known disaster in the garment industry was the Rana Plaza factory collapse in Bangladesh on April 24, 2013, which resulted in the death of over 1,100 people and injured over 2,000. This unsafe facility was the site where many Western retailers had their textiles manufactured. Constituting the worst garment factory collapse ever, it received significant media coverage. In the immediate aftermath of this tragedy, multinationals from around the world lined up to defend their reputations, many arguing that they did not know that conditions were so bad.

The disaster led to calls for Western retailers, and manufacturers more generally, to be far more transparent about their global supply chains. By disclosing the facilities where their products are produced, they could no longer hide behind "ignorance". Rather, disclosing their suppliers would incentivize these Western retailers to ensure working conditions were up to their stated standards, and when that is not the case, either push suppliers to improve those standards or seek alternatives.

There are many such initiatives to enhance supply chain performance. One well known initiative is led by Human Rights Watch called *Follow the Thread: The Need for Supply Chain Transparency in the Garment and Footwear Industry.* This initiative pressures companies in the industry to adopt a Transparency Pledge, which involves the publication of names and addresses of factories that supply these retailers, the number of employees in those factories, as well as some additional information. According to *Follow the Thread*, such a declaration would constitute an important step in making retailers accountable to those who work in the facilities that produce the goods that they sell.

Such challenges extend to many other industries as well. For example, there is significant pressure being placed on food companies to provide more transparency in their supply chains, with stakeholders demanding information about the treatment of animals, the use of chemicals, impacts on the environments where they operate, and child labour. Chocolate companies have

received significant negative attention, with Hershey, Nestle, Cargill and others facing child slavery charges in the United States, brought about through a lawsuit launched by a human rights group, related to business practices on Ivory Coast cocoa farms. While these

While the importance of shareholders as a stakeholder group is still crucial, the interests of other stakeholders cannot be ignored. Fortunately, these two perspectives are increasingly aligned.

companies eventually won a dismissal in U.S. courts, it did have reputational implications.

There is also a very recent case in the UK, where in July 2023, a Scottish court ruled against a tea company which is headquartered in Scotland. The court is allowing a legal case to move forward where 2,000 workers in Kenya are seeking damages for suffering which they claim resulted from poor working conditions. The court's ruling highlights the risks UK based companies have for their business practices in other countries.

The Legal System

Increasingly, companies, including members of their boards of directors, are facing legal challenges. According to a leading Canadian law firm, Torys, "The range of claims that may be advanced by stakeholders is wide and can relate to a variety of ESG issues, including efforts to address diversity and inclusion in organizational leadership, and failure to properly prepare for the future impacts of climate change." Accordingly, "Companies can mitigate the risks of ESG litigation by adopting regular audits of foreign operations, internal training, and meaningful grievance and remediation protocols."

3. ESG is not just a challenge: it can be an opportunity when approached correctly

The primacy of shareholders has been the dominant paradigm in corporate finance for many decades – that is, the fiduciary responsibility of corporate officers has traditionally been to shareholders alone. Firms deploy strategies to maximize profitability, and with that, shareholder value.

Increasingly, however, this view has been shifting – in Canada, the supreme court has ruled that legal obligation of corporate officers is to the corporation. While the importance of shareholders as a stakeholder group is still crucial, the interests of other stakeholders cannot be ignored. Fortunately, these two perspectives are increasingly aligned.

The pathway to maximizing shareholder value has evolved. Efforts to improve working conditions for employees inside the organization and along the supply chain leads to many benefits that enhance organizational performance. Deploying strategies that reduce

Efforts to improve working conditions for employees inside the organization and along the supply chain leads to many benefits that enhance organizational performance

carbon emissions reduces environmental impacts that are clearly having a negative impact on many businesses and society overall. Being systematic in deploying strategies that lead to more diverse and inclusive work environments has been shown to enhance innovation, employee engagement, and performance.

As noted in the seminal paper by Michael E. Porter and Mark R. Kramer entitled Creating Shared Value,

> *"In recent years business increasingly has been viewed as a major cause of social, environmental, and economic problems. Companies are widely perceived to be prospering at the expense of the broader community.... A big part of the problem lies with companies themselves, which remain trapped in an outdated approach to value creation that has emerged over the past few decades. They continue to*

Strong ESG performers manage not only the full spectrum of those environmental, social, and governance factors that are material to their businesses, but also recognize and address their interdependence.

view value creation narrowly, optimizing short-term financial performance in a bubble while missing the most important customer needs and ignoring the broader influences that determine their longer-term success... Companies must take the lead in bringing business and society back together... Businesses must reconnect company success with social progress. Shared value is not social responsibility, philanthropy, or even sustainability, but a new way to achieve economic success. It is not on the margin of what companies do but at the center. We believe that it can give rise to the next major transformation of business thinking."

Conclusion

ESG has become the driving force of corporate value. Strong ESG performers manage not only the full spectrum of those environmental, social, and governance factors that are material to their businesses, but also recognize and address their interdependence. ESG is not a form of corporate advocacy for any one outcome, but a strategic response to the rapidly evolving market in which a business operates. ESG connects the business and scientific transformations happening today with the reforms in politics and institutional structures required to achieve a systems-based approach to creating value.

Companies that appropriately identify, assess, prioritize, manage, and report on ESG factors will gain a competitive advantage over peers.

Andrea Barrack is the Senior Vice President, Corporate Citizenship & ESG at RBC and the Executive Director of the RBC Foundation.

Walid Hejazi is a Professor of Economic Analysis and Policy at the Rotman School of Management.

Susan McGeachie is co-founder and managing partner at Global Climate Finance Accelerator and an adjunct professor of climate finance with the University of Toronto.

A fully referenced version of this article is available on request from editor@dl-q.com

Dr Rosina Watson

Leading for Sustainability

became Head of Corporate Responsibility at Argos, the major UK retailer, in 2008, when our forward-thinking CEO, Terry Duddy, recognized the need for a senior leader to consider and manage the company's wider environmental and social impact. It was around the time that Mike Barry launched Marks & Spencers' pioneering Plan A, and Paul Polman set out Unilever's Sustainable Living Plan. Terry asked me to do the job because I knew the business operations and people well having had eight years' prior experience in the company across finance, strategy and commercial roles.

It was an amazing role. Finding ways to make the business more successful, at the same time as reducing our negative impacts, and even creating positive value for society gave me a renewed purpose. There were so many opportunities to be more efficient, to waste less, to help our customers and motivate our colleagues by thinking

Managers must now respond to the changing needs and expectations of a wider set of organizational stakeholders

about planet and people as well as profit. Everywhere we looked there were opportunities to reduce cost, increase efficiency and improve our reputation. It just made good business sense and accordingly we called our sustainability programme "The Basis of Good Business."

But it was also an extremely challenging role. Seeing the opportunities was one thing but making them happen was another. I had held senior roles before, but this one had some added dimensions: 1) it involved technical knowledge, but also softer skills such as influencing and storytelling; 2) it was much more outward looking, with more time spent talking to people outside the business, including competitors; 3) it was about challenging assumptions and the status quo, driving innovation and change and 4) hardest of all, it involved changing the narrative around what it meant to be a good business, and how to achieve and measure that.

I left Argos in 2013 to embark on a PhD at Cranfield which allowed me to become an academic. I thought I could have more impact as an individual by teaching others how to take their organization down a more sustainable path, and since 2019 I have led Cranfield

School of Management's fast-growing Sustainable Business group.

But what capabilities do managers need to contribute meaningfully to a more sustainable future? And how can these be taught?

The case for education for sustainability

In the face of global social and environmental challenges, there is increasing pressure from customers, investors, and citizens for business to be part of the solution. The British Academy's Future of the Corporation project defines the purpose of business to be "to profitably solve problems of people and planet, and not profit from causing problems" (The British Academy, 2019). This means that managers must now respond to the changing needs and expectations of a wider set of organizational stakeholders, in the context of a volatile, uncertain, complex and ambiguous (VUCA) environment. They need to lead their organizsations in ways that contribute to solving society's challenges rather than adding to them and play their part—in their value chains, communities, industry sector and wider society—in achieving systems change.

However, most organization, tend to find it difficult to manage towards measures of success beyond profit. They tend not to be very good at looking outside their boundaries to tackle problems that are not within their

Most organizations tend to find it difficult to manage towards measures of success beyond profit. They tend not to be very good at looking outside their boundaries to tackle problems that are not within their direct control, or that require partnership and collaboration to solve

direct control, or that require partnership and collaboration to solve. Many professionals do not have the skills to make this complex and unchartered journey towards more sustainable business practices. As individuals, we can find it difficult to imagine the radical changes we will have to make in the way we live, work and do business if we are to bring human activity back into balance with the wider living world.

Sustainability education literature speaks of an urgent need equip managers with the competencies they need to transform management practices and lead their organizations towards a more sustainable future. This includes contributing to achieving the 2030 Sustainable Development Goals and the Paris agreement's commitment to achieve Net Zero by 2050, as well responding to an ever-expanding set of sustainability-related regulations and reporting frameworks. We need leaders across all functions of business who are capable of working collaboratively to address complex sustainability challenges.

Addressing these shortcomings requires education that "empowers learners to take informed decisions and responsible actions for environmental integrity, economic viability and a just society, for present and future generations, while respecting cultural diversity" (UNESCO, 2020). Higher Education Institutions

(HEIs) have a pivotal role to play in offering sustainability education that equips leaders to respond to their rapidly changing organizational contexts. This is particularly the case at postgraduate level, where many mid-career professionals return to study, full time or alongside their work. HEIs are attempting to embed sustainability into their missions and curricula, guided by international frameworks like the Principles for Responsible Management Education (PRME) initiative, and the inclusion of sustainability criteria into accreditation frameworks (e.g. AAACSB and EQUIS). There is certainly growing pressure for this from management students; a study by Yale Center for Business and the Environment found that 70% of business students want more experiential learning focused on sustainability; and 65% desire more case studies highlighting sustainability issues.

Competencies for sustainability

There is some consensus now emerging around the competencies for sustainability that need to be taught. As far back as 2011 Wiek, Withycombe and Redman synthesized the evidence on the required competencies for sustainability into a framework outlining the knowledge, skills, and attitudes necessary for successful task performance and problem solving with respect to real-world sustainability challenges and opportunities

It is clear from the research that sustainability skills and competencies are just as much about personal agency, influencing, leadership and critique of 'business as usual' as they are about applicable knowledge and skills to deliver more sustainable solutions.

in businesses and management. It is composed of five key competencies which must be integrated to success-fully co-create knowledge and action for sustainability. These are:

- systems-thinking competence
- anticipatory competence
- normative competence
- strategic competence
- and interpersonal competence.

More recently in 2021, Advance HE/QAA published its Education for Sustainable Development Guidance setting out eight key competencies for sustainabil-ity, based on UNESCOs key competencies for sustain-ability, which themselves build on Wiek et al's seminal framework.

These competencies need to be taught and learnt though holistic, transformational learning approaches, because they demand relational learning and a questioning and evolution of people's values and belief systems.

Research by the United Nations and global people advisory firm, Russell Reynolds (see DLQ36 article: **Sustainable Leadership**) identified four comparable critical capabilities which, when coupled with a sustainable mindset, underpin sustainable leaders' success. These are:

- multi-level systems thinking
- stakeholder influence
- disruptive innovation
- and long-term activation.

Teaching sustainability competencies

It is clear from the research outlined above that sustainability skills and competencies are just as much about personal agency, influencing, leadership and critique of 'business as usual' as they are about applicable knowledge and skills to deliver more sustainable solutions.

So, what have we learnt at Cranfield about teaching these competencies?

First, you need *interdisciplinarity*. Leading for sustainability requires technical skills, but also management

and leadership skills. You need to know how to measure a carbon footprint, but you also need to be able to drive a programme of change to reduce it. This means breaking down the silos between climate scientists and future CEOs so they can understand each other's language and combine their knowledge and perspectives. For example, Cranfield's Sustainability Business Specialist Apprenticeship is the first ever Cranfield course to be owned and delivered by two schools (School of Management and School of Water, Energy and Environment) bringing together natural and social scientists working on sustainability research more closely than ever before. It also means teaching people from many different business functions about sustainability, not just the sustainability/ESG team. At Cranfield, this means embedding sustainability into other management disciplines through new modules such as Economics for Sustainability, Personal Leadership for Sustainability and Sustainable and Circular Supply Chains.

Next, you need *diversity*. Diversity in cognition, knowledge, expertise, and perspectives are critical to create the necessary and urgent solutions to the societal challenges we face as a global community. As well as considering diversity within your workforce, this also means empowering people to look outside the organization to see how others in your sector are responding to sustainability challenges, and working with competitors, suppliers and other societal actors (e.g. government, non-profits) to address systemic challenges. Learners on our Sustainability Business Specialist Apprenticeship come from diverse disciplines (from engineering to finance), with different levels of prior education; they work in private, non-profit and government organizations

This also means empowering people to look outside the organization to see how others in your sector are responding.

in sectors from defence to social housing. We create as much space as possible for them to learn about, and from, each other, as well as from the course team, and this is widely recognized as contributing to the development of critical competencies including systems thinking, stakeholder engagement and collaboration.

Strategic sustainability. All too often, sustainability is seen as a tick-box exercise, a cost, or a distraction from core business. To counteract that, a powerful thread throughout our sustainability teaching is conceptualizing sustainability as a core element of strategic formulation and execution. As Julie Owst, who is Head of Sustainability at Bidfood, a leading UK food wholesaler, and a Cranfield Sustainability Business Specialist Apprentice explained:

> *"When I started in the role, I was trying to hit everything in the UN Sustainable Development Goals, which is 17 goals. Rosina did a module on leading sustainable business which made me realize I need to do a materiality assessment and really look at how our business model is relevant to sustainability. The idea is to focus on less but*

Systems thinking is increasingly recognized as a core competence for sustainability, but it notoriously hard to teach on an accelerated timescale.

> to do more in that area. It's improved our prioriti-
> sation, and our whole strategy has then changed.
> The business is then seeing the value that we're
> delivering commercially too."

Underpinning this, is the ability to identify and implement *value creating innovation*. Tools such as our Sustainable Value Analysis tool help managers to challenge the status quo and benefit from their collective diversity of thinking and understanding of stakeholders' perspectives to envision product and business model innovation which creates environmental and/or social as well as economic benefits. It's when sustainability initiatives generate value – for customers, for employees, for communities, and for the bottom line, that energy and momentum can be created.

Systems thinking is increasingly recognized as a core competence for sustainability, but it notoriously hard to teach on an accelerated timescale (it usually comes from experience!). Teaching systems thinking is not just about shifting thinking to a holistic viewpoint, but about helping managers to develop their understanding of the impacts and unintended consequences of decisions, both within their value chains and beyond into a sector or global ecosystem. There is also a need to help leaders consider *much longer time horizons* than is typical in business strategy cycles, to consider multiple possible future scenarios that may unfold, and the risks and opportunities they present to their organizations.

One way we engage learners in systems-thinking with a long-term perspective is through a role-playing game which takes participants on an experiential, transformational journey to 2050. During the game, players representing established businesses interact with players representing entrepreneurs, policymakers, civil society organizations and citizens as they all react to changes in economy, technology, and society along alternative pathways towards a more sustainable future by 2050. The 'winners' are judged not only by the resources they accumulate, but by whether they have achieved their purpose. Participants reflect on the world they have collectively created through their beliefs, values and actions. They are encouraged to apply this learning to strengthen their leadership in the present.

Cranfield facilitated a half-day game-play experience for the management team of environmental service company, Lucion Group, intended to help the company align day-to-day decisions with its sustainability/ESG goals and group purpose. After playing the game, the management team experienced an immediate 20% uplift in their belief that they could contribute to sustainable futures as individuals and a 16% uplift in their belief that they could do this together as an organization. Both figures increased by a further 3% in the six months after the learning experience. Participants in a follow-up focus group attributed this increase in agency to the understandings, awareness and relationships developed during the game. As Jeremey Meredith, Managing Director of Lucion Services reflected:

"The game was a truly immersive experience. It was thought-provoking and insightful and absolutely helped everyone who participated understand the scale of the challenges we face. Importantly, it helped us all to consider what we could do within Lucion Group to reduce our dependency on carbon. The message was clear, we must take action to hit and exceed carbon reduction targets by 2050 to safeguard our planet."

Developing sustainability competencies in your organization

With reference to the Cranfield Leadership for Sustainability competency framework, which distils the compe-

Box 1: Eight competencies for sustainability

SUBJECT KNOWLEDGE AND KNOWLEDGE OF ALL SDGS

COMPETENCE[1]	A STUDENT WHO DISPLAYS THIS COMPETENCY CAN:
WAYS OF THINKING	
Systems thinking	· recognize and understand relationships · analyse complex systems · consider how systems are embedded within different domains and scales · deal with uncertainty
Anticipatory	· understand and evaluate multiple outcomes · create their own visions for the future · apply the precautionary principle[2] · assess the consequences of actions · deal with risks and changes
Critical thinking	· question norms, practices and opinions · reflect on one's own values, perceptions and actions · take a position in the sustainable development discourse
WAYS OF PRACTICING	
Strategic	· develop and implement innovative actions that further sustainable development at the local level and further afield
Collaboration	· learn from others (including peers, and others inside and outside of their institution) · understand and respect the needs, perspectives and actions of others · deal with conflicts in a group · facilitate collaborative and participatory problem solving
Integrated problem-solving	· apply different problem-solving frameworks to complex sustainable · development problems · develop viable, inclusive and equitable solutions · utilise appropriate competencies to solve problems
WAYS OF BEING	
Self-awareness	· reflect on their own values, perceptions and actions · reflect on their own role in the local community and global society · continually evaluate and further motivate their actions · deal with their feelings and desires
Normative competency	· understand and reflect on the norms and values that underlie one's actions · negotiate sustainable development values, principles · goals and targets, in a context of conflicts of interests and trade-offs, uncertain knowledge and contradictions

1 Based on the UNESCO/AdvanceHE/QAA framework.

2 A broad approach to innovations with potential for causing harm when extensive scientific knowledge on the matter is lacking, emphasising caution, pausing and review.

I HAVE LIVED THROUGH THOUSANDS OF FUTURES.
I HAD EXPECTED TO LIVE THROUGH YOURS.

Your sustainability strategy should be tightly aligned or integral to your core business strategy.

tencies outlined above, I will close with some practical suggestions of ways to build sustainability competencies in your leaders and your organizations.

Strategic sustainability. Your sustainability strategy should be tightly aligned or integral to your core business strategy. You cannot expect a small group of sustainability experts to 'look after' sustainability while the core business continues as usual. Sustainability is not just about the technical aspects of measurement and reporting of impacts. It is about changing the narrative around what your organization is there to do and the value it creates and being able to win over the hearts and minds of your employees, helping them see how they can contribute to this. Think deeply about how you integrate sustainability into governance and core activities including strategy development, procurement, and financial reporting.

Stakeholder engagement. Many organizations are hiring from other industries, or even other sectors to increase their ability to understand and work with their stakeholders, including non-profits and even same-sector competitors. Deeper engagement with customers can be achieved through co-creating ideas and prod-

Cranfield Leadership Competencies for Sustainability (David Grayson and Rosina Watson)

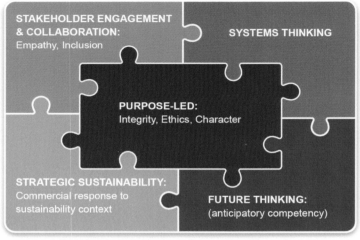

STAKEHOLDER ENGAGEMENT & COLLABORATION: Empathy, Inclusion

SYSTEMS THINKING

PURPOSE-LED: Integrity, Ethics, Character

STRATEGIC SUSTAINABILITY: Commercial response to sustainability context

FUTURE THINKING: (anticipatory competency)

Coach – Communicator – Connector - Champion

ucts, for example, through crowdsourcing. Volunteering and secondments can provide opportunities for employees to widen their understanding of and empathy with stakeholders.

Systems thinking. Participation in cross-functional projects and in industry-sector coalitions can offer employees a wider view of your organization's ecosystem.

Future thinking. Finding ways to bring in the voice of younger generations can provoke longer-term thinking. Some companies are building 'shadow boards' comprised of younger, next generation leaders who can offer this perspective. Setting longer-term company and personal targets can also help.

Purpose orientation. Activating a purpose beyond profit in your organization can unleash the energy and creativity of your team in support of your sustainability strategy. Setting this wider purpose is a first step, but bringing it to life is the key, and this means connecting employees' personal purpose to the wider purpose of your organization. Some companies find B Corp accreditation useful – this involves a change to a company's articles of association to explicitly allow directors to consider the interests of all stakeholders, not just shareholders, when making important decisions. A new ISO 37000 standard outlines how to govern for purpose.

Dr Rosina Watson *is Associate Professor of Sustainability at Cranfield School of Management. She is Head of Cranfield School of Management's Sustainable Business group, Co-director of the Sustainability MSc and co-creator of the Sustainable Futures game (***cranfield.shorthandstories.com/sustainablegame***). She was formerly Head of Corporate Sustainability at Home Retail Group, which followed 15 years in finance, strategy and commercial roles.*

Read more about Sustainability at Cranfield School of Management in our latest Principles of Responsible Management Education (PRME) report.ds

A fully referenced version of this article is available from editor@ dl-q.com on request.

Natalie Beinisch and
Deborah Edward

Managing Complexity and Leading Change

Building the Circular Economy in Nigeria

The Circular Economy Innovation Partnership (CEIP) is an organization based in Lagos, Nigeria. Our company was founded in 2020 with the aspiration to build circular business and investment opportunity in the country.

2020 was a particularly tough year. In Nigeria, a country where unemployment rates reach over 30%, and where waste management infrastructure is creaking under the weight of a skyrocketing population, the economic impact of the Covid-19 pandemic crushed hopes of recovery from a 2016 recession. The concept of a circular economy is that goods are designed, manufactured, consumed, and disposed of with the goal of eliminating or minimizing waste. It promises both locally driven diversified economic growth and simultaneous environmental protection. At least conceptually, the Circular Economy offers a panacea to some of Nigeria's existential problems.

There are also global ramifications: Nigeria claims one of the world's top spots when it comes to waste leakage into oceans

Driven by economic necessity, Nigerians are inherently "circular": the market for second-hand computers is particularly notable, with a highly organized private market that produces qualified refurbishment engineers and supports entrepreneurship. Likewise, materials such as scrap metal are recovered and recycled at very high rates through informal and formal networks.

However, amid exceptional examples of entrepreneurialism are some difficult realities. International trade of second-hand products has meant there are high volumes of unusable goods including e-waste and textiles entering the country from developed markets. This leads to very dire consequences if these materials are not treated properly. Dyes and chemicals are particularly harmful when leaked into the environment, exposing communities to very serious air and water pollution. There are also global ramifications: Nigeria claims one of the world's top spots when it comes to waste leakage into oceans.

Interestingly, "Circular Economy", defined as a set of business practices, was introduced in Nigeria under a different pretext: developed countries were trying to address over-consumerism through technological innovation in the West and their interest to recycle and reuse unwanted products while promoting bilateral trade in developing economies/global south. While laudable, this approach to the Circular Economy is not entirely compatible with the needs and interests of Nigerian business and society.

It is important to distinguish what the Circular Economy is in general terms and what it means in terms of promoting Nigerian interests. Thus, when we think about Circular Economy in Nigeria, there are three important factors to consider. This includes:

1. Circular Economy as an idea that supports local economic development
2. The translation of ideas into organizational practice
3. Knowledge, talent and access to resources

Our work at CEIP has focused on developing programs around these themes in what we hope are constructive ways that contribute to a larger global agenda to promote the Circular Economy and a more local agenda to create meaningful economic and professional opportunity.

Circular Economy to Support Local Economic Development

Circular Economy is a tool to support local economic development because the business models it advocates such as sharing platforms, products-as-a-service and industry symbiosis are both more economically and environmentally efficient to manage at a local level. For example, it is harder to share manufacturing assets when businesses are not co-located. Because economic growth is so important in Nigeria, particularly in terms of creating value-added services locally, circular business models are very exciting.

It takes hard work and investment to determine how to minimize or extract value from waste in a way that is commercially viable.

Unfortunately, it is not that easy to build circular business models. It takes hard work and investment to determine how to minimize or extract value from waste in a way that is commercially viable. Furthermore, because the organizations that produce and commercialize waste are often different, coordination is very important to translate waste into revenue streams. This is why we developed LOOPLab, an open innovation program in partnership with the German Agency for International Cooperation (GIZ), the Netherlands Enterprise Agency (RVO), Lagos State Government and many private sector organizations including Coca-Cola, BASF, Nigerian Breweries and the Food and Beverage Recycling Alliance of Nigeria to support the development of local businesses and their linkages to larger organizations.

Our first program focused on packaging waste. Together with our partners, we identified two areas of opportunity for circular business development connected to recovery and recycling of packaging waste and conversion of waste into other types of consumer products. An example of a partnership that was nurtured through this program was between Nigerian Breweries and Eco-Circular Solutions. With a zero-waste policy, Nigerian Breweries sought to identify an off-taker for paper labels that were removed from bottles at its facilities as they were prepared for re-use. Eco-Circular Solutions, on the other hand, is a start-up focused on manufacturing ceiling tiles from recycled paper and cardboard. By matching the two companies and supporting them in the process, Eco-Circular Solutions was able to reduce its input costs of manufacturing by acquiring waste paper from one large scale industrial producer in order to produce ceiling tiles.

The LOOPLab program also includes a research fellowship. In working with companies to define open innovation challenges, a key learning was that many of their challenges were unrelated to the technology or business models but structural issues that undermined the commercial viability of circular models. For example, one company raised the issue of pricing for PET bottles, which was volatile and deterred entrepreneurs from entering the market. Our decision to build the research component of LOOPLab was based on the view that we cannot be in a position to successfully build circular business models in Nigeria if these types of elephants in the room are ignored. We also believed that by engaging with universities on salient issues, we are able to support the development of locally relevant applied research. While we believe the Fellowship program was highly successful, alumni are now working directly with the entrepreneurs participating in the program, it underscores that commercially viable circular business models remain out of reach to organizations that do not have access to substantial investment, motivated consumers or strong regulatory incentives.

As we have extended our work in open innovation to fibres, e-waste and construction materials through our partnership with Innovate UK-KTN, our lessons are the same: there are some examples where circular business models are potentially viable, such as with eco-design of buildings, but it is more likely the case that a lot of ground-work and collaboration across different sectors is needed to identify and build meaningful local business opportunities. As this work is essential, we are doubling down on our efforts to build the ecosystem and develop the networks and relationships that are needed to transform latent opportunities into actual ones.

Ideas are like prom dates: elegant as the night begins, but increasingly more unkempt and unruly as the night goes on.

Translation of ideas into organizational practice

As we have underscored, Circular Economy approaches are alluring. Ultimately the concept of Circular Economy is that we can create value by reducing waste and respecting the environment. In a context where the impacts of climate change are more real than ever, it is hard not to be drawn in by this promise. Unfortunately, ideas are like prom dates: elegant as the night begins, but increasingly more unkempt and unruly as the night goes on.

In working with businesses in recycling sectors, we learned that consumer behaviour was a critical factor that affected the costs of collecting materials at their end of life. It is fairly common in Lagos for consumers to litter on the streets and practices such as source segregation are relatively unheard of. Sadly, it is vastly more costly to collect waste that has been spread across the environment and its worth is substantially lower. Thus, while in principle, waste can hold value in terms of its potential to be recycled or converted into new products, this value is much more inaccessible when waste is not disposed of or managed properly.

Working with the recycling community, we learned of the role that facility managers could play to change consumer behaviours, as they are responsible for the way that tenants and employees channel their waste. Surprisingly, although some companies have strong recycling programs in Nigeria, there are very few facility managers either at the industry or residential level that have designed and implemented recycling and resource management programs. This is because there is nothing really motivating them to do so as there is no stringent enforcement and set-up can be costly in terms of time and money. For some waste streams such as electronics, operating a recycling program can even incur costs.

Based on our understanding of the critical role played by facility managers, we developed the "True Leaders Programme" together with Lagos Business School. The idea behind the program is that "true leaders" sometimes have to make and execute decisions that are not easy, even if the long-term benefits of those are positive. Forty facility managers participated in the program, many of whom were at the beginning of setting out a recycling and circular economy strategy.

The program kicked off with a needs assessment, to help us understand the motivations and development needs of potential participants. Through this assessment we learned that many types of facilities, from residential estates to industrial complexes, were indeed interested in setting up recycling programs. However, because a number of different organizations are responsible for managing different types of waste streams in Lagos, many were unsure of who to contact. Many organizations also indicated they had negative experiences with waste collectors, as they often did not show up when they were expected. Another challenge shared in this assessment was that it was difficult to convince tenants to separate their waste, making it harder to implement recycling schemes.

Based on this assessment, we developed a three-day curriculum that focused on change management and on improving linkages between the public and private organizations that oversee waste management. A post-program follow-up was also designed to track progress and continue to support facility managers to implement recycling programs.

While the *True Leaders Programme* is a small intervention, it is a demonstration of how important it is to identify and nurture interactions across a wide range of stakeholders to build the viability of even what seems a most straightforward business model. Given that many circular business models require even more changes on the part of producers and consumers, it is important not just for facility managers, but all types of "true leaders" to invest in external relationships in a deep and reflective way.

Knowledge, Talent and Access to Resources

Global changes in technology and organization mean that the jobs of tomorrow may be substantially different than those of today. Circular Economy business models are centred on technological and digital innovation and on changes in economic organization. In a scenario where universities and company-based talent management programs are well-equipped to respond to change, the question of how to equip the next generation with all the relevant skills and knowledge to navigate an increasingly complex and interdependent world is a tough nut to crack.

In Nigeria, universities and businesses are not well equipped: R&D spend is a fraction of that in developed economies and large swathes of academic talent have emigrated. While there are many progressive organizations in the country, the business environment is one often characterized by firefighting, where issues such as talent development and future-proofing are luxury areas to address. This is very bad for Nigeria, as the skills gap strangles productivity and competitiveness.

Our work to build the Circular Oasis community, a group of students and young professionals that have an interest to develop their careers on Circular Economy themes, is an example of the type of effort that can be made to lower costs of talent search and development for organizations working in the circular economy space.

The origins of the Circular Oasis community are from the LOOPLab program, as students participating in it requested to continue to build as a group. The group is evolving into a self-governing organization that is structured to develop both soft skills such as communications, leadership, empathy and trust and hard skills such as logistics, lifecycle analysis and material composition analysis that are needed to grow circular businesses and organizations. Through the Circular Oasis community, we have placed young talent in our partner organizations, lowering their search and onboarding costs.

The question of how to equip the next generation with all the relevant skills and knowledge to navigate an increasingly complex and interdependent world is a tough nut to crack.

Furthermore, by developing materials such as management case studies that are centred on local businesses, we also work with local universities to create teaching resources that are both high quality and address relevant business issues faced by Nigerian managers and founders.

While we are in the early stages of building a young and vibrant talent pipeline, we are unshakeable in our belief that Nigeria's youths and young enterprises deserve substantial investment in their professional development and that this will pay off not only in terms of producing technical skills but also supporting the development of a collaborative and open mindset that is essential to creating meaningful business opportunity in Nigeria and internationally.

Leading Sustainable Change in Complex Environments: Learning from the Circular Economy in Nigeria

Based on our work at CEIP, we draw three lessons:

1. An important aspect of complexity is that motivations of different organizations to cooperate are not the same. Circular Economy in developed economy contexts is a reaction to consumerism, while in developing economies motivations are to optimize investment in economic growth. Regardless of the issue, different motivations should be recognized in any environment to allow diverse organizations to explicitly define their own agendas, while achieving collective goals.

2. Leaders continue to make increasingly difficult choices as they deal with unprecedented levels of uncertainty and ambiguity. They must continually navigate contradictory pressures to deliver shareholder and public value. In this environment, intentional and genuine reflection by leaders about the meaning of value and the investments that are needed in external relationships is exceptionally important.

3. Investment in talent should not overlook the latent potential of young professionals in developing markets. As the cost of acquiring and retaining talent is increasing, leaders must be creative in their efforts to build learning and development opportunities for individuals inside and outside of their organizations. With advances in learning technology, the time is ripe to take advantage.

The Circular Economy is an idealized vision of functional interdependence between diverse organizations.

The Circular Economy is an idealized vision of functional interdependence between diverse organizations. Implementation of Circular Economy concepts however reveal that there are competing interests between organizations that must coordinate, contradictions about value creation and entrenched behaviours on the part of consumers and businesses that constrain change. While the Circular Economy is a niche area, it is nonetheless representative of the complexity faced by leaders in contemporary organizations. Through our own efforts to build Circular Economy business opportunities and those of others, we can and should learn how to navigate complexity more reflectively.

Natalie Beinisch *is Executive Director of Circular Economy Innovation Partnership. Her previous work has centered on sustainable finance and leadership development. She earned her B.A. from McGill University and her PhD from the London School of Economics.*

Deborah Edward *is Communication Manager of Circular Economy Innovation Partnership. A graduate of Linguistics, UNIBEN, she is actively involved in the development of programs that promote capacity development and access to jobs for youth, business communications strategy and social impact.*

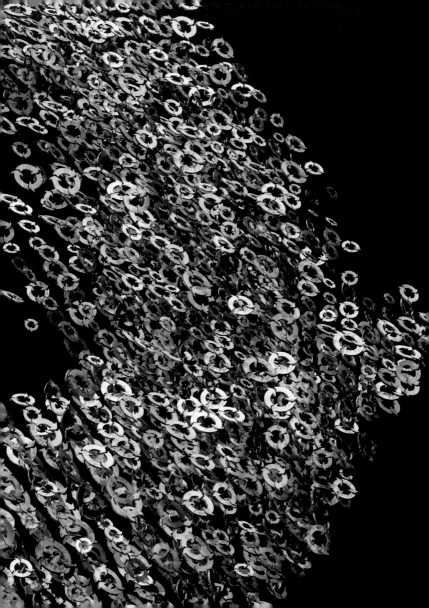

Melea Press

The Burden
of Doing
Sustainability

While top organizational leadership is typically involved in creating a sustainability strategy, the enactment of the sustainability strategy happens by other employees inside an organization. This work gets distributed across the organization and is most often quickly passed out of top leadership hands and into the hands of the workers.

Some organizations have resources to hire new sustainability managers or create new internal positions. In these privileged organizations, an individual has been clearly identified and has explicitly agreed to the take on this role. In some cases, new sustainability managers have experience with what this means in terms of building multistakeholder teams, creating and working toward benchmarks, collecting data, writing and filing reports, and reporting back to other leaders.

More typically, the burden of enacting sustainability strategies is dispersed across employees who happen to be around or happen to have something to do with the focus of the strategy. Many of the organizations I have worked with have inadvertently put enormous pressure on their employees by failing to understand what it means for individuals when responsibility for sustainability action is given on them. Individuals tend to be excited about activities they can contribute to that in turn have positive outcomes for society and the environment. This initial enthusiasm can support the efforts that the actual work requires, and can cause awkward dissonance as those doing the work become exhausted but feel they *should* still be excited about the opportunity. I have seen this play out in the same ways across organizations.

In a large DIY business, a quality assurance manager became responsible for verifying factory adherence to their new and developing sustainability standards. The QA manager was used to looking at products, usually in domestic warehouses, not determining adherence to standards inside foreign factories. The demands being placed on the QA manager to learn multiple new skillsets were enormous. He had to understand, and in some cases develop, the sustainability policies for foreign factories, to figure out how to support foreign factories in meeting those new standards while knowing of horror stories around the secondary effects of factories firing women, and to learn how to communicate with the factories so that the amount of his new orders aligned with the

Typically, the burden of enacting sustainability strategies is dispersed across employees who happen to be around or happen to have something to do with the focus of the strategy

rates of their compliant output. The new skills needed to enact the sustainability standards became a burden placed on this QA manager. He had to figure out how to document, report and communicate these activities internally and externally to the organization.

At a transport business, the manager who oversaw trucking fleets was given the new responsibility of monitoring greenhouse gas (GHG) emissions for the organization. They had to figure out how to monitor the trucking fleet, which was most likely straight-forward, as this was part of their current job. However, they also had to identify other sources of GHG emissions from the fans and forklifts in their factories to the engines running the conveyor belts, and this task is complex. Very complex. It involved people and parts of the organization the trucking manager did not know. It meant gaining an understanding of how to keep track of these various people and measurements. It meant being able to understand what the measurements meant and being able to incorporate them into one ultimate number than could go into a report. all while still maintaining their original job.

While eager employees may be initially thrilled to take on sustainability responsibilities, this can change as the reality of the work piles up over weeks and months

The person responsible for maintenance at a local authority became responsible for transitioning to environmentally-friendly internal ordering. She had to seek new suppliers who carried a full line of environmentally-friendly products that were needed and negotiate new prices. These may be unwelcome changes, but well within her area of expertise. What was not in her area of expertise was what to do about shortfalls when her budget would not be increased to reflect the increased pricing she faced. She had to look across the whole organization to see where cuts could be made and where savings could be found. She determined that some savings could be made through behaviour change of people using the facilities, and thus a campaign was needed. This was not within her initial skillset.

The burden of enacting sustainability comes in different ways. For many, their job descriptions are dramatically expanded or completely changed with no warning. This increases the amount of work they need to do and expands the knowledge and skills they need to do their jobs.

The stress of adapting to new responsibilities in a role is made more complex when the role includes anything around sustainability. Employees are learning new knowledge, new frameworks, and new skills *on top of their other work.* While eager employees may be initially thrilled to take on sustainability responsibilities, this can change as the reality of the work piles up over weeks and months, and progress reports need to be written, supply chains need to be audited and tracked, external input needs to be collected and addressed, progress needs to be documented, annual reports must be published, etc.

Short-term thinking will not accomplish long-term goals. One of the reasons industries known for not being sustainable, such as tobacco and oil and gas, have adopted sustainability initiatives is so that they can gain access to better employees

This is further exacerbated by the drudgery of sustainability reports. Collecting data and writing a report is a lot of work. Creating sustainability reports that will adhere to European Sustainability Reporting Standards (ESRS), the Global Reporting Initiative (GRI), or other reporting frameworks, is a massive undertaking with a steep learning curve. These reports take months to fill out and often are partially graded on completeness, which means having issues and items in their intended places – something that is not always clear. Those who can afford the luxury hire others to help them learn how to fill-out the forms because they are both difficult to understand and cumbersome to complete. These reports may be separate from other industry-specific reports, and hopefully your organization will create its own sustainability report that reflects a more personal and person-oriented, narrative look at your sustainability efforts. Regardless of the report type, the work of sustainability reporting is extraordinarily time consuming. This is not new. Increased workloads happen when there is a transition to monitored activity. Agricultural producers face barriers in transitioning to organic because the paperwork is endless. The auditing industry faced increased workload after the ENRON scandal in 2001 led to new, increased monitored activities and new standards. In a similar way, writing sustainability reports, seeking sustainability accreditations or labels requires increased work.

There exists an idea in Western societies that "doing sustainability" is a good thing, and thus, the people who get to do this work should be happy; employees should be thrilled when the organization they work for adopts a robust sustainability initiative. There is an expectation that employees should and will feel so appreciative to have their job imbued with this layer of meaning that they will not complain about the extra work. Afterall, individu-

Your employees harbour a wealth of life experience that normally does not come to light at work; this is an opportunity to let some of their expertise come to light.

als should be honoured to be chosen or invited or given the opportunity to be part of a sustainability initiative. Their jobs are made more meaningful when individuals get to contribute to sustainability; employees should be proud and happy that we have meaningful work. In reality however, this just leads to burnout.

Employees may choose to take on sustainability projects in their organization because of the personal boost it gives them. However, when they are not compensated for the additional projects and must work into the evening or on the weekends to stay on top of their normal work, the benefit of the sustainability project must be called into account. It could be that the project has a huge return on investment to your organization, your sustainability strategy, and your stakeholders. If this is the case, workloads need to be adjusted to reflect this value. Overwork, even for a noble cause, is not acceptable, not sustainable, and does not adhere to ideas of Fair Work. If your sustainability strategies are to be taken seriously and accomplish long-term goals, they must be enacted within human limitations.

Short-term thinking will not accomplish long-term goals. One of the reasons industries known for not being sustainable, such as tobacco and oil and gas, have adopted sustainability initiatives is so that they can gain access to better employees. These industries rely on the desirability brought by their sustainability work to entice people, who otherwise would not have considered a position in such a company. Third sector organizations dismiss expected low wages, something associated with the type of work they are doing.

Sustainability strategies can drive organizational and personal growth and value and behaviour change, or they can suck the lifeblood out of already exhausted people who were just looking to focus on something more meaningful at work. Burnout is not a good reward for doing the work of sustainability.

Celebrating learning from each other and learning from the process is a powerful tool to encourage engagement and ownership.

Supporting ongoing engagement with your sustainability strategy

Guidance and resources are needed to be successful – this most likely will come from outside your organization. You cannot do this alone. The employees you have tasked to enact your sustainability strategies, likewise, cannot do it alone. This could mean going to conferences or workshops to gain missing skills, or creating working groups across organizations within the communities where you work, or online across others who work in your industry. Collaboration and learning exchange are both necessary for you to thrive.

Too often doing sustainability gets pushed down to mere auditing and reporting, rather than highlighted as an exploration into the process of new kinds of engagement, transformation and impact. Many organizations place too much emphasis on reports, forgetting to identify the stories of the real people who have headed the work within the organization, the engagement with other stakeholders, and the experiences and outcomes that have been created as a result of great effort. Taking time to highlight the narrative of how something was accomplished or who did something brilliant that caused a pivotal change will lead to greater engagement inside the organization, and greater legitimacy for your position as an organization on a sustainability journey outside the organization.

Employees engaged in doing sustainability can be supported by creating a platform for them to share their learnings across your organization. This is different from knowledge sharing or exchange. Learning exchange refers to the knowledge, the things they have learned, and how they have applied that information to different problems. Sharing knowledge does not necessarily spark innovation, however, sharing learning allows people to see where they might apply similar solutions, or how similar solutions could be adjusted to address issues they are facing in their work. Enabling learning exchange highlights and celebrates the new expertise employees have developed, and also invites others to share their own experiences. Your employees harbour a wealth of life experience that normally does not come to light at work; this is an opportunity to let some of their expertise come to light. Learning exchange is about making space for growing enthusiasm for lifelong learning within your organization and celebrating it.

In addition to publicly acknowledging the work those doing sustainability inside your organization have been engaged in, creating opportunities for learning exchange outside your organization – within your industry or community – will increase the impact of your sustainability strategy. Further, these learning exchanges will create opportunities for you to document your impact in a variety of experiential ways – from photographs and videos of events to creative works of art and design or innovation that emerge from these exchanges. This is one way your organization can become a catalyst for broad positive impact.

As you develop learning exchanges, encourage the individuals who are deeply engaged in doing sustainability within your organization to share their process, not just the outcomes. Encourage them to share what they don't know, what they worry about, and what went wrong in their journeys to the positive outcomes you celebrate. Celebrate all participants, by name and contribution if they are comfortable with this, and encourage each participant to celebrate their collaborators and the people who inspired and encouraged them. Take time to tie these celebrations back into the main parts of your sustainability strategy, the value proposition of your organization, and the high-level goals you are working toward.

Celebrating individuals builds a culture of inclusion, agency, and continued engagement with your sustainability strategy. Celebrate the individuals in your organization and who are learning new frameworks and skills, taking on new activities, exploring the edges of their comfort zones, and innovating together.

The first place to start is making your sustainability strategy a creative journey. Make sure it is understood that everyone in the organization is on a journey together

Everything must be linked directly to the big goals you laid out for how your sustainability strategy enacts the value proposition of your organization

How can I engage every person in my organization on this creative journey?

Engage in a creative journey. The first place to start is making your sustainability strategy a creative journey. Make sure it is understood that everyone in the organization is on a journey together, and identify clearly the agency you are offering. If you can offer support in terms

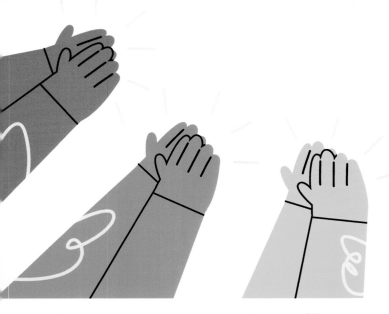

of time, budgets, materials, make that clear. Most important is that you demonstrate over and over that creativity
and initiative are celebrated, and whatever the outcome
– a success, a failure – you are prepared to learn and
adapt and iterate. I have seen awards for biggest fail,
praise for best insight from a failure, presentations on
multiple failures that ultimately led to a great innovation.
Celebrating learning from each other and learning from
the process is a powerful tool to encourage engagement
and ownership.

*Invite the "unheard" and marginalized to have a
central voice.* Inviting those who don't typically come
forward to participate in your sustainability journey

Celebrating learning from each other and learning from the process is a powerful tool to encourage engagement and ownership

can have transformative results for your sustainability journey, your organization, and their individual life journey. Making a specific call to those who are not already engaged is critical. Think carefully about whose voices are often unheard in your organization. You may have done work around Equity, Diversity and Inclusion in your organization, which points to key elements to consider including race, religion, LGBTQI+, transgender, hidden disability, visible disability, people over 50 or under 30, seniority in the organization, and intersectionalities. If you have not done serious EDI work, do note that there is growing evidence showing that diversity yields, unsurprisingly, more innovative, and better results. However, it must also be noted that inclusion takes cultural work. Inviting people to be 'included' without making it possible will cause self-doubt and greater uncertainty and can be considered 'gaslighting'. If you have not done this cultural work to make space for diversity in your organization, please do it now – yes, right now. This is not just "soft" skills, this is not hiring policies, this means creating a culture where everyone feels they belong and can contribute and develop personally and professionally; this is a social sustainability issue.

Celebrate learning from each other. Create opportunities for learning exchange sessions where people engaged in the work of sustainability, or interested in a particular topic can share their personal experiences and knowledge with each other. Include seemingly "odd" mix of people and let them share across their silos. Celebrate the process and communicate clearly about the process. Make sure these "process updates" are shared and celebrated internally.

Expect to iterate

You can do this. You can develop a sustainability strategy that aligns with your value proposition, your organizational goals and your personal goals. You can bring your organization, and your industry along. You can bring energy and ideas and impact into your orga-

Create opportunities for learning exchange sessions where people engaged in the work of sustainability can share their personal experiences and knowledge with each other.

nization. You can transform in any way you want. It will take work, so make sure the work is aligned with the vision, make sure the work is focused on a shared goal, and by all means, make sure that no one person takes it all on, takes it on alone, or heads toward burnout. A creative journey means embracing the unknown, celebrating and learning from successes and failures, and supporting each other. Focusing on metrics and reports is a route to failure. Focusing on people, positive impact, and the joy of collaboration, learning from each other and ultimate transformation is your route to success.

Melea Press *is an Associate Professor at the* **University of Glasgow** *Adam Smith Business School and Chief Policy Officer at* **The Undaunted***. For the past 20 years she has focused on sustainability in social systems, markets and communities; exploring social and cultural systems, and the individuals who make up those systems.*

A fully referenced version of this article is available from editor@ dl-q.com on request.

Sofia Appelgren

Leading in an Inclusive Way for a Socially Sustainable Future

n 2008, as I gazed upon my 10-week-old child, I made a profound choice. I decided to delve deeper into the intricacies of our global society, to question the biases that stem from birthright and privilege. I pondered, why do we judge before we truly understand? What can we learn beyond the confines of societal norms and the teachings of our education? What is a product of fear? I asked myself "How on earth are we going to live together in peace <u>thanks</u> to our differences..."

Our world is filled with irrationalities that defy logic and hinder progress towards the society we envision. To effect meaningful change, we must think globally and act locally, shifting individual behaviours one step at a time.

With this burning curiosity I embarked on a remarkable journey with nothing more than commitment and engagement to start with. In 2008, I laid the foundation for my first venture with a purpose – to spread knowledge, expand boundaries, raise awareness about diversity and inclusion issues, and provide a platform for people to connect. It was a journey that would require time, unwavering commitment, and an unyielding dedication to making a positive impact. And it has taken me to over 20 countries over the last 15 years, to societies and communities where people are treated unfairly, without privileges and support to have the equal and fair prerequisites in the labour market as the norm. We have learnt a lot...

Our world is filled with irrationalities that defy logic and hinder progress towards the society we envision. To effect meaningful change, we must think globally and act locally, shifting individual behaviours one step at a

time. It will not be a quick fix, but it is doable. And we are experiencing a big shift at the moment. Never before have so many organizations embraced DEI and never before are so many leaders actively working on finding their purpose to drive a meaningful change far beyond the company that they are responsible for. This is a really positive sign.

In this journey, collaboration is paramount. It takes collective action, the strength of many voices, and the creation of platforms for those voices to be heard. It takes many positive voices to balance one negative, and an incredible determination to be that positive voice that never falters.

It takes many positive voices to balance one negative, and an incredible determination to be that positive voice that never falters.

To move forward effectively, we must unite colleagues, customers, suppliers, and stakeholders with a shared purpose and agree on the betterment of our world, our communities, and our businesses. To bring a company onboard on this journey we need:

- **A Shared Vision:** craft a shared vision embodying sustainability as a core value, a vision that provides the company with a clear northern star which will help keep the work on the right path. The energy company Vattenfall, has a clear vision, engaging all the executive management, with a rolling D&I officer position in the executive team this, keeps the shared vision living through the various business areas within the company.
- **Open Communication:** foster open dialogue, where every voice is heard and ideas flow freely, all voices, Stena Metall, the recycling company, have during 2023 started up a new cross-functional multi-country inclusion and diversity group to do just this. Lifting the voices of the company with the CEO listening actively to pave the way for the change which matters.

- **Inclusive Leadership:** embrace diversity and inclusivity in leadership. Volvo Cars' 375+ leaders trained in inclusive Leadership from 2017-2020. Both formal and informal leaders, developing and practising inclusion in the everyday makes substantial change. Giving these leaders tools helps to further the impact.
- **Education and Awareness**: invest in continuous education and awareness campaigns. Deloitte Sweden has ongoing DEI training throughout the various business areas which started with the their own CEO joining the "CEOs for D&I" program in 2021 – training covers areas such as the basics of DEI, inclusive recruitment, cultural awareness, etc as just some examples of how Deloitte is raising knowledge which is in turn leading to change. Also, Ingka Group, IKEA's holding company, has been working hard to build competences internally to better understand biases and how they affect business processes. Over 3,000 leaders have so far taken their unconscious bias training and Ingka Group are committed to having 70% of all leaders complete it by the end of the fiscal year. To date, over 700 senior leaders have completed DEI training, starting with group management, then followed by country and function management teams across key Ingka Group markets.
- **Transparency:** share information on sustainability goals openly and widely, let everyone feel them and enjoin them to do their part. Axel Johnson, the

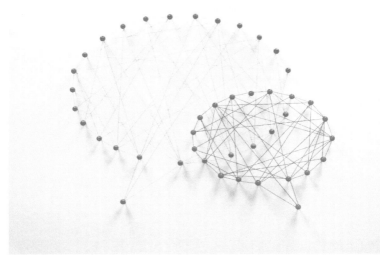

family-owned company, has shared their D&I goals both internally amongst the group and externally, to both inspire others and hold themselves accountable. This paired with their inclusion survey to measure progress is providing the transparency needed.

- **Collaboration Platforms:** create platforms for collaboration and learn from others, we grow together by sharing knowledge. Collaboration platforms are hugely scaleable, the one we operate has around 2000 people a year participating in it. It is a mentorship platform that shares knowledge regarding norms, unconscious bias and organizational culture. Mentors get access to the platform and lots of ways to exchange experiences as well as their

Be the support and change by reaching out and engage in the societies in which you operate (ACT local)

journey with mentees. The results have included increased job opportunities for mentees who have previously struggled to find a job; more empathy and a deeper understanding of those who struggle; and more ideas on how to act more inclusively; it is also a tool for the organizations to pick up and highlight role models and new learning to increase the overall inclusion in the workplace.

- **Incentives and Recognition:** reward sustainability efforts, highlight role models, for example many the of the companies and universities working with mentorship that we know, do storytelling about their mentorship journeys, inspiring others to also be a mentor and highlight their efforts internally.

- **Long-term Commitment:** demonstrate unwavering dedication. Send signals that "this is here to stay". In 2021 Cevian, an active ownership investment firm, released a statement on incorporating ESG metrics into the senior management compensation plans for European public companies. Improving companies ESG performance and situation is a clear and important source of long-term value creation.

- **Goal-Setting and Monitoring:** set clear, measurable sustainability goals. "What gets measured gets done", for example, Axel Johnson have Diversity and Inclusion goals that affect all the companies that they own. These are long-term and it have had a huge effect on cultural mindsets, with impact being seen in the actions taken and results such as innovation and talent attraction. When you know it's a "diverse friendly company" there is also potential to be yourself which increases the chances of higher wellbeing and performance.

- **Product Innovation:** invest in sustainable product development through diversity and with an inclusive mindset. For example, innovative companies that have embraced more diverse thinking and can access a broader market reach in their research experience more valuable testing results.

- **Local Community Engagement:** engage with local communities and build partnerships that benefit both parties. Listen to community concerns, contribute positively to local development, and involve them in sustainable initiatives. Be the support and change by reaching out and engage in the societies in which you operate (ACT local), The organizational partners we have worked with have, through community engagement, been able to find well-educated foreign-born academics who had skill sets far above their current job roles, that they can bring onto their staff. They have also enabled under-privileged youth to overcome barriers to further studies and so enter the job market and engage in the wider culture. Clearly it is not only the Partners that benefit from this; by supporting next generation employees to be more included, but also the whole of society can benefit with this kind of support and inclusion,creating the right initial conditions for more to enter meaningful work.

- **Advocacy and Policy Support:** advocate for sustainability-friendly policies at local, national, and global levels that supports your community to grow. A group put together by the Swedish government that I was privileged to be part of, has been discussing how the Swedish public sector can better cooperate with companies and NGOs for better longterm results. The true objective is to continuously learn from each other and support each other to lower barriers for a common purpose.

The approach aligns with the social dimension of ESG, which emphasizes a company's social responsibility, diversity, inclusion, and community engagement. Here is how to connect those elements:

- **Diversity and Inclusion:** create a strategy that aligns with the ESG "S" with a clear vision and goals that promote diversity and inclusion both within companies and in society through programs that aim to support vulnerable or underrepresented groups while bringing the company to a new level of awareness and purpose.
- **Skills and Talent Development:** harness the skills and talents of underrepresented groups, such as immigrants and refugees.
- **Networking and Collaboration:** facilitate connections between universities, researchers, companies and social movements through different platforms such as network meetings, podcasts, seminars, or annual symposia. It enables companies to engage with communities, address social issues, and contribute positively to society, thereby fulfilling their social responsibilities.

Some Examples from Practice

In-House Training Inclusion and Diversity Initiatives: We have created dedicated training programs to build awareness among employees. This not only benefits employees but also aligns with ESG's social dimension by promoting a diverse and inclusive workplace.

Internship Programs: SEB, Sweden's largest bank, has created internship programs that allow immigrants and refugees to gain work experience in Swedish companies. The internships are connected with Sweden's

Harness the skills and talents of underrepresented groups, such as immigrants and refugees.

largest mentorship program for people with foreign background who lack a job that match their qualifications. This creates not only valuable opportunities for immigrants but also helps companies tap into a diverse talent pool, aligning with the social aspect of the "S" in ESG.

Cross-Sector Partnerships: Axel Johnson supports community development and social movements, supporting initiatives that address social issues such as education, integration, or poverty alleviation. It is a great way for companies to leverage their resources and their influence to support social causes.

Advocacy and Awareness: it is also important to advocate for policies and practices that promote diversity and inclusion in the corporate world, to raise awareness about the importance of social sustainability and the role of businesses in contributing to positive social change.

When the CEO of Deloitte or Head of Strategy at AB Volvo are mentors to people who fight for a job but lack the crucial networks and knowledge of the local labour market, it sends signals of engagement and commitment. When an entire HR department decides to broaden their talent pipeline by becoming aware through addressing unconscious biases and norms, and challenge their processes, it will give more of the company's talent a better chance to reach the job they are looking for. When leaders act more inclusively it leads to innovation, because internally more people feel 'seen and heard' and dare to raise their voice and feel safe. When an investor starts to set up clear requirements on how their potential investment should serve to take on a social responsibility and approach DEI, we will start moving the needle. When the CEOs in our designed program "CEOs for D&I" decided to give space to DEI, they found a personal purpose to drive the "S" and it truly made a difference.

The mission for our organizations is to create transparency about social inequities and to build trust. When new generations with an awareness of DEI benefits enter the labour market, it strengthens not only the requirements of sustainable reporting (CSRD[1]) it also heals an ever more divided world that currently gives us less chance "to be the change we wish to see". Let's be inspired by the "social entrepreneurship world" where empathy and purpose are at the heart of what drives us. Imagine every company embracing the "S" in a genuine way. It would address unhealthy societal tensions and make for a much better world for more people.

We often repeat the old African saying in our workplace, "If you want to go fast, go alone; if you want to go far, go together". In unity and collaboration, we hold the power to shape a sustainable future, one where our actions today lay the foundation for a brighter tomorrow.

Sofia Appelgren is the founder and boardmember of Mitt Liv AB and the Mitt Live Foundation, two social enterprises that work for an inclusive society and a job market that values diversity. She holds Board positions with impact investor, Destination Invest Gothenburg AB and the NGO, Engineers without Borders. (**www.mittliv.com/se**)

---

1 Corporate Sustainability Reporting Directive (CSRD) and the interlinked European Sustainability Reporting Standards (ESRS) Read about it in the EU website: https://tinyurl.com/y69tmuww

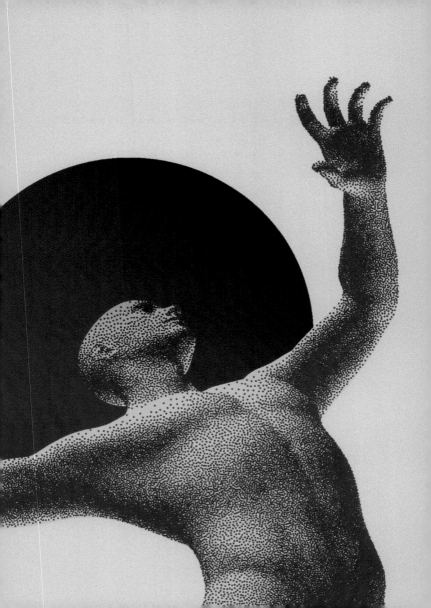

Doreen Ankrah
with contributions
from Jamie Bristow
and Daniel Hires

Inner Development Goals

Inner Growth for Outer Change

n an era where attention to external factors and mecha-
nistic solutions often takes precedence, the concept of
Inner Development Goals (IDGs) emerges as an innovative approach for communicating the value of personal
growth to collective sustainability and systemic change.
Unlike conventional goals that focus solely on material
gains, the IDGs delve into the realm of integrated development, encompassing emotional, psychological, social,
and spiritual well-being to better equip us for the unprecedented challenges we face today.

Rooted in extensive interdisciplinary research, the premise is straightforward: without a foundational shift in human values, understanding, and leadership capacities, external solutions may prove to be too slow, inadequate or short-lived. Whilst the IDG Framework is itself innovative, the IDG organization that co-created it has consistently adopted a creative approach to addressing some of the most pressing challenges of our time.

A Contextual Overview

The dawn of the 21st century brought with it an acute realization of the multifaceted challenges that the global community faces. Recognizing the pressing need for a cohesive and comprehensive strategy, in 2015, the United Nations introduced Agenda 2030. Central to the agenda lies the inclusive set of 17 Sustainable Development Goals (SDGs) - targets for a future where everyone has an equitable opportunity and our planet's health is restored and preserved.

Having just passed the halfway point to this deadline, the unfortunate reality is that progress has so far been disappointing and is still far off track. Data released in the 2023 Sustainability Development Report shows that based on the current pace of progress, less than 20% of the SDG targets are on track to be achieved. In fact, it indicates that we are further off-track than four years ago as

Our evolutionary history, which has us primed for immediate threats and short-term decision-making, often falls short when confronted with long-term, abstract problems.

a consequence of the ongoing pandemic, rising inflation and the cost-of-living crisis, planetary, environmental and economic distress, along with regional and national unrest, conflicts, and natural disasters.

While possessing the necessary resources and technology to achieve the goals, considering the SDGs solely as technical problems solvable through structural policy instruments or other external methods might be contributing to our lack of progress. The SDGs provide a tangible roadmap, but a crucial question arises: do humans currently possess the capacity to navigate this intricate and interconnected landscape of challenges?

Our evolutionary history, which has us primed for immediate threats and short-term decision-making, often falls short when confronted with long-term, abstract problems. The complexity of our modern environment and societal issues often outstrips our innate cognitive capacities, triggering our unconscious psychological barriers such as denial, rationalization or discordance, among other 'dragons of inaction'.

Addressing our global challenges necessitates a change in the underlying mindsets that originally caused them. It requires an innovative approach to identify, rectify and reshape the fundamental origins of these issues - human behaviour. Fortunately, modern research shows that the inner abilities we need to face and overcome these complex challenges can be developed. This was the starting point for the Inner Development Goals initiative.

Bottom Up and Inside Out

Personal growth and development are by no means new concepts in humanity's history - ancient civilizations and religions have long recognized their importance. Whilst

Has the fast-paced nature of today's world impacted the time and importance allocated to self-reflection and inner development? And most importantly, in what ways can we reintegrate these principles to address contemporary challenges and enhance well-being?

interpretations and practices differ across cultures and belief systems, personal growth, ethical conduct, and inner development have been cross-cultural and enduring aspects of human life for millennia. What has gone astray in our modern relationship to these fundamental concepts? Has the fast-paced nature of today's world impacted the time and importance allocated to self-reflection and inner development? And most importantly, in what ways can we reintegrate these principles to address contemporary challenges and enhance well-being?

Answers to these crucial questions begin to emerge from the broader history of personal growth movements and psychological approaches, such as humanistic, transpersonal and positive psychology, that have sought to investigate human well-being and inner development since the Industrial Revolution. A particularly illuminating perspective, and one that has been instrumental

One of the Nordic retreat centres - Vasterberg Folkhögskola, 1890 - picryl.com

in shaping the IDG initiative, can be gleaned from the cultural, historical, and philosophical underpinnings of Nordic societies - renowned for their unique approaches to governance, education and welfare.

In the book *'The Nordic Secret'* Lene Rachel Anderson and Tomas Björkman (one of the coo-founders of IDG) describe in detail how the Nordic countries transitioned from poor, agricultural and authoritarian societies in the 1860s to wealthy, industrialized democracies just a few generations later. This remarkable transformation was achieved due to the facilitation of personal development in the state-sponsored – but not state-organized – retreat centres all over the Nordic countries.The retreat centres were located in nature, away from the complexity of rapid social change. Here, young adults

In times of uncertainty and rapid change, the only way to build truly stable societies is to build them from the bottom up and from the inside out, with real change beginning in the mind - both collective and individual

could spend up to six months with the expressed goal of finding their inner compass and becoming active co-creators of the emerging new social order. At the turn of the 19th century, there were approximately 100 retreat centres like this in Denmark, 75 in Norway, and 150 in Sweden, with up to ten per cent of each generation of young adults participating in these programmes.

The authors present a compelling argument for re-evaluating traditional models of societal development and governance. Echoing the Nordic principles of self-awareness, community cohesion and sustainable growth, they call for a greater focus on human development, empathy, trust and cooperation as crucial elements for building sustainable and harmonious societies. They propose that in times of uncertainty and rapid change, the only way to build truly stable societies is to build them from the bottom up and from the inside out, with real change beginning in the mind - both collective and individual.

The aim was to synthesize a complex field of inner development into a simple framework that helps to name, understand, communicate and facilitate the 'inner' changes that are needed for an 'outer' change to occur

The Emergence of The IDGs

The inspiring insight behind the formation of the Nordic retreat centres was somewhat forgotten over the course of the 20th Century. Fortunately, in recent years, there has been a growing focus on the notion of inner transformation and related methodologies for societal change. This heightened interest is evident across various domains, such as sustainability science, education and policy-making, as demonstrated by the growing number of academic articles dedicated to the topics of inner development and sustainability progress. Reflected in the literature is the urgent need for more integrative approaches that link sustainability's inner and outer dimensions to facilitate transformation at various scales, including the individual, collective, and systemic levels.

Between 2019 and 2020, a significant undertaking took place on Ekskäret Island within the Stockholm archipelago. During this period, a group of adult development scholars, which included prominent figures like Otto Scharmer, Amy Edmondson, Peter Senge, Jennifer Garvey Berger, and Robert Kegan, collaboratively authored and endorsed the *'Growth That Matters Manifesto'*. The manifesto, serving as a call to action, highlighted the pressing need to work systemically with human growth in adults in order to better meet the accelerating complexity of societal challenges.

Amidst these developments, the Ekskäret Foundation, in collaboration with the 29k non-profit organization and The New Division, led by founder Jakob Trollbäck, who notably led the design of the iconic SDG logos, engaged in concerted efforts to advance this innovative approach to confronting the world's 'wicked issues'. These initiators established connections with various stakeholders, including companies, researchers, and other interested parties aligned with the IDG project's vision. The aim was to synthesize a complex field of inner development into a simple framework that helps to name, understand, communicate and facilitate the 'inner' changes that are needed for an 'outer' change to occur.

A series of meetings were organized with founders, CEOs, HR managers, sustainability managers and influential figures in both the private and public sectors, as well as many discussions with researchers and leaders from prominent academic institutions in Sweden. With collaboration, they succeeded in formulating a key survey question that could collect as much relevant input as

The IDG Framework is primarily pedagogical. First and foremost it's a communications tool for the conceptualization and cultivation of inner developmental capacities.

possible on which skills and qualities are most important in order to work more effectively towards the SDGs.

Shaping The IDG Framework

The IDG global survey activities, forming the basis of the IDG framework, involved three innovative phases. Phase 1 developed and distributed the survey in March 2021 to capture the varied insights from people with a professional relationship to sustainability issues. Participants were asked which *'abilities, qualities or skills are essential to develop, individually and collectively, to get us significantly closer to fulfilling the UN Sustainable Development Goals'.* After analysis and iteration, 23 skills were identified and, in order to have a more pedagogical framework, organized into 5 dimensions.

Phase 2, developing the toolkit, engaged over 3000 collaborators, including world-leading scientists, educators, organizations and government representatives. The toolkit is an evolving, open-source project that provides free and practical tools grounded in scientific research, helping individuals and collectives to develop each of the 23 skills.

To reduce any Western-centric bias and ensure the framework's global applicability, Phase 3 of the research is currently in progress. The latest survey aims to reach over two million people and is anticipated to yield 100,000 responses from more than 100 different nations. The survey opens-up the co-creation to more voices in a well-structured, inclusive and truly global dialogue that will shape the future of the IDG Framework.

Unveiling The IDG Framework

The intended function of the IDG Framework is primarily pedagogical and is, first and foremost, a communications tool for the conceptualization and cultivation of inner developmental capacities. The Framework uses purposefully simple language that is comprehensible and effective for practitioners to incorporate the IDGs into their respective governments, organizations, institutions or personal lives. The idea is that establishing this framework will draw interest, foster engagement, and spur further development with collaborative partners and institutions.

This innovative and collective endeavour aims to popularize and integrate these crucial skills into diverse aspects of individual and societal life. The Framework is a map that can assist us in navigating the landscape of our inner lives. It identifies areas of growth so that we can better handle complexities, deepens our connection to ourselves, others and the world, and fundamentally enhances our effectiveness as change agents and leaders, paving the way to a more sustainable future.

To provide a better understanding of each of the 5 dimensions, a small description accompanies each one, explaining their distinct attributes and significance:

Being: Cultivating our inner life and developing and deepening our relationship to our thoughts, feelings, and body help us be present, intentional and non-reactive when we face complexity.

The IDG Framework covers 23 skills, organized into 5 dimensions.

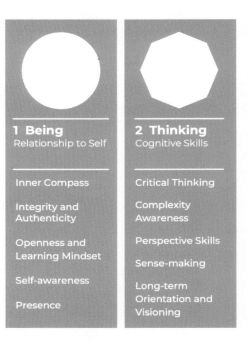

1 Being
Relationship to Self

Inner Compass

Integrity and Authenticity

Openness and Learning Mindset

Self-awareness

Presence

2 Thinking
Cognitive Skills

Critical Thinking

Complexity Awareness

Perspective Skills

Sense-making

Long-term Orientation and Visioning

Thinking: Developing our cognitive skills by taking different perspectives, evaluating information and making sense of the world as an interconnected whole is essential for wise decision-making.

Relating: Appreciating, caring for and feeling connected to others, such as neighbours, future generations or the biosphere, helps us create more just and sustainable systems and societies for everyone.

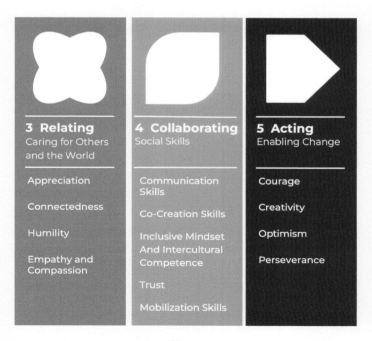

3 Relating
Caring for Others and the World

Appreciation

Connectedness

Humility

Empathy and Compassion

4 Collaborating
Social Skills

Communication Skills

Co-Creation Skills

Inclusive Mindset And Intercultural Competence

Trust

Mobilization Skills

5 Acting
Enabling Change

Courage

Creativity

Optimism

Perseverance

The focus of the IDGs provides an overarching view of global challenges, with the IDGs zeroing-in on both the individual and collective role within larger systems

Collaborating: To make progress on shared concerns, we need to develop our abilities to include, hold space and communicate with stakeholders with different values, skills and competencies.

Acting: Qualities such as courage and optimism help us acquire true agency, break old patterns, generate original ideas and act with persistence in uncertain times.

When positioned alongside other frameworks, the unique focus of the IDGs becomes evident. While many developmental strategies, like the SDGs, provide an overarching view of global challenges, IDGs zero-in on both the individual and collective role within these larger systems. It is not a replacement for broader frameworks but rather a complementary perspective, emphasizing that macro-level change is inextricably linked to micro-level transformations.

A potential criticism that emerges is the interpretation of the term 'inner' within the IDGs and its framework. There is a common misconception that 'inner' solely pertains to individual introspection and personal qualities. Whilst it is true that the term implies individual personal growth and self-awareness, when applied to broader contexts, 'inner' can also encompass the core values, principles, culture and ethos of collectives and organizations. This broader definition emphasizes the importance of aligned group dynamics and the interconnection of personal and collective growth in driving systemic change.

A further criticism of the framework is the perceived subjectivity of the 23 skills. While frameworks like the SDGs provide quantifiable targets, the IDGs' emphasis on inner qualities and personal growth can be seen as less tangible. How does one measure self-awareness or empathy without depending on self-reports? Can such intangible goals be universally applied, given the diverse cultural and societal contexts across the globe?

Such questions continue to be addressed through discourse and research, but it is essential to recognize that the strength of the IDG Framework lies in its flexibility. While it offers a map for inner growth, it does not prescribe a one-size-fits-all approach, nor does it represent a training curriculum in itself. Its simplicity is a design principle, both keeping it easy to communicate and relatively 'naked' or decontextualized, ready to be re-contextualized within specific training or personal development approaches. This adaptability allows it to be tailored to diverse cultural and societal contexts, ensuring its relevance across different settings. By recognizing its limitations and continuously refining the framework in response to feedback, the IDGs can become an increasingly robust and globally transferable tool in the quest for a sustainable and equitable future.

Practical Applications and Implications

The IDGs work in four main areas: Communication, Movement Building, Policy Development and Research, which are vital in disseminating the message and strategies of the IDGs to a broader audience. Similarly, the primary stakeholders working with the IDGs are companies, NGOs, governments and academic institutions because of their vast potential to facilitate collective learning and drive systemic change.

In pilot countries, such as Costa Rica, where ministers have formally adopted the IDG framework, collaborative efforts with IDG Country Centres have been initiated to develop and strengthen leadership capacities across various sectors, ensuring a more integrated approach to sustainable development that includes both external and inner dimensions.

Multinational corporations like Google, Ikea, and Ericsson are among the first collaborating partners to incorporate IDGs into their corporate frameworks.

Multinational corporations like Google, Ikea, and Ericsson are among the first collaborating partners to incorporate IDGs into their corporate frameworks and intentionally work on the inner skills needed for sustainable change within the company. However, using the IDG Framework to help leaders perceive the wide range of cognitive, emotional and relational capacities that will help them to take on challenges and better contribute to sustainable development is just the first step.

The IDG initiative, as a whole, facilitates the systematic development and application of critical inner skills in a variety of other ways: by offering leadership workshops and masterclasses, working closely with agents of change within organizations and governments, and providing an annual summit where participants can immerse themselves in transformative experiences, engage with experts, and collaborate on innovative solutions for personal growth and societal advancement.

At an individual and community level, the IDG team/initiative organizes monthly online gatherings that act as the steady heartbeat of the global community; it empowers individuals around the globe to start their own IDG hubs (currently over 350), connecting the community based on the shared understanding of the IDG Framework, and finally, it provides an open-source online toolkit with more than 30 evidence-based approaches that individuals and teams can use to cultivate each of the 23 skills.

Looking Forward

The IDG initiative, having been established in 2020, is at its beginnings, yet its influence on the global landscape is already significant. As recognition and acceptance of the Framework spreads, the potential for further transformative impact is exponential. With the commitment of change agents, both in positions of influence and among everyday citizens, the IDGs are capable of catalyzing positive shifts on personal, communal, and global levels.

The journey ahead is not without challenges, as the dynamic nature of global ecological issues necessitates continuous adaptation and innovation. By emphasizing the symbiotic relationship between individual growth and societal progress, the IDGs offer a novel perspective on the path to ecological sustainability. The challenges

Inner development is not a supplementary activity to be pursued once all other tasks are completed, nor can external systemic changes wait until the inner work has been done. It is best understood as a continuous and collective process of inquiry, growth and learning through action.

we face as humanity are an invitation - an invitation to rethink, reimagine, and rebuild; to consider who we need to be in this next chapter of civilization. The IDGs serve as a compass in this journey, pointing towards a future where individual transformation drives societal progress.

This is a call to action for researchers, policymakers, educators, practitioners, and readers alike to consider exploring and applying the IDGs within their professional and personal spheres. Inner development is not a supplementary activity to be pursued once all other tasks are completed, nor can external systemic changes wait until the inner work has been done. Both are mutually reinforcing and should not be seen as competing demands. Furthermore, inner development is not a journey to be undertaken alone or as a one-off; rather, it is best understood as a continuous and collective process of inquiry, growth and learning through action. Only by cultivating our inner capacities can we hope to overcome the multitude of challenges before us, ensuring that our outer achievements are firmly rooted in inner wisdom and resilience.

*This article was written by **Doreen Ankrah** (Marketing Coordinator), with contributions from **Jamie Bristow** (Policy and Advocacy) and **Daniel Hires** (Director of Partnerships and Marketing). In keeping with the spirit of IDG, this article is a testament to co-creation and collaboration, made possible by every member of our organization, partners, and community.*

Inner Development Goals *(IDG) is a non-profit organization for inner development that. Its mission is to research, collect, and communicate science-based skills and qualities that help us to live purposeful, sustainable, and productive lives. Supported by a growing community of practitioners, researchers, organizations and governments, IDG seeks to bridge the gap between personal growth and global transformation. A version of this article was originally written for Veolia's FACTs report in Fall of 2023.*

www.innerdevelopmentgoals.org

Rolf Pfeiffer

How to Address Sustainability in the C-Suite?

n starting, let me posit that higher levels of sustainability in our work environment will significantly increase employee engagement, one of the most important drivers of the success of an organization. Higher levels of sustainability will only prevail if there is a "tone from the top" supporting this idea. Only then can we hope that higher levels of sustainability will "trickle down" through the organization and reach most leaders, managers, and employees as key elements of good business practice.

However, while we all like to use the word "sustainability", and probably associate something rather positive with it, I am not sure that we have had a good conversation in our organizations on what we mean by "sustainability": is it financial, environmental, life balance? "Sustainability" is one of those terms that many people can project a lot onto, and unless the conversation to come to an agreement on what "we mean by it" happens in earnest it can be very fuzzy.

Without the "tone from the top", increasing levels of sustainability in organizations is even more demanding than it would otherwise be. Hence, exploring the topic of sustainability in the C-Suite – using a wide-angle lens – is a worthwhile endeavour.

First up, we have to ask: "why is sustainability of leadership roles important?", "how can it contribute to the success of our organization?".

Dealing with Individuals

"We often forget that we are dealing with individuals who perversely try to behave as human beings" Peter Drucker said of leaders in organizations and the people they lead.

The 20th century has been dominated by theories and practises that derive standards of good leadership

"Sustainability" is one of those terms that many people can project a lot onto, and unless the conversation to come to an agreement on what "we mean by it" happens in earnest it can be very fuzzy.

from hierarchical organizations, with military organizations as an important reference. Douglas McGregor's Theory X is an example of that and has been replicated in the vast majority of factories. Early impulses to create more sustainable conditions were driven by highly inspired factory owners but did not become a general trend. It can be argued that in many countries, certainly east and west of the North Atlantic, trade unions have contributed to creating more sustainable conditions for deskless workers over time, with quite a bit of work still to do, no matter where we look.

However, to answer the questions posed at the top of this piece, we need to look to today's organizations and their development. What stands in the way of these places being properly sustainable for their people and leaders? Factors include competitive pressures, short-term demands by shareholders, lack of resources, inadequate leadership and management practises and, at the highest echelons of leadership, quite a bit of ego.

Raising levels of sustainability is ever more important these days, as many economies face acute shortages of talent across many sectors. One result of this development is that companies that do not pay attention to changing values in the target employee populations risk no longer being able to attract the quality and quantity of people needed to sustainably manage their businesses going forward. Too many business leaders have not yet understood this dynamic. If your target employee population wants more sustainable careers, and you don't offer that to them, they will move elsewhere and make your competitors successful.

Turning an idea such as increasing sustainability across the board into a reality requires deep conviction and powerful champions who will drive this idea forward even against opposition, and it requires courage and perseverance to make it work. It will be easier to implement when the main shareholders of a company are deeply convinced of the merit of this approach. Therefore, we see an opportunity for companies with dominating or majority shareholders (often family-owned companies) leading the way. Very few are ready to take bold decisions as Paul Polman did within his first month of being named CEO of Unilever: he announced that Unilever would stop quarterly reporting with immediate effect, as quarterly reports did not support the pursuit of more mid – to long-term plans, and he invited shareholders who were not happy with this decision to take their invest-

"We often forget that we are dealing with individuals who perversely try to behave as human beings"
Peter Drucker

ment money elsewhere. Imagine doing that at any time of your tenure as CEO of a listed company – let alone in the first month.

He clearly decided to switch off the autopilot, to leave the beaten track, to go against the grain – use the image you fancy most. He could have been inspired by an approach consisting of seven steps to success, after being willing and able to acknowledge autopilot(s) driven by habit, by emotions or by entrenched positions, and then to switching them off and finding more mindful answer to key questions.

1. Taking the time to understand the situation and focus on what might be at stake, without jumping to conclusions straight away – *listen to really understand each other*. (Mindfulness)
2. Understanding the purpose of what is/what might be – what is it that higher levels of sustainability system might help us achieve? And *what happens if nothing happens?* (Why?)

3. Seizing the opportunity to look at the situation from as many vantage points as possible – what *do higher levels of sustainability look like from a leader, a manager, an employee, a customer, a family member, a shareholder perspective?* (Perspective)

4. Clearing away the assumptions and beliefs, grounding the situation in facts and mutually recognized decision-making criteria, *creating a shared reality – that all involved can agree on.* (Reality)

5. *Investigating the options available and inspiring action* to get to the decisions needed – whether this ends up being a "do nothing" decision or the launch of a large-scale cultural transformation program. (Investigate)

6. Staging *the activities needed to move from status quo to desired next level*, and creating time boundaries that marry the time and space to consult all stakeholders with a clear timeline to action. There is a time to switch from consulting and listening to deciding and acting. (Staging)

7. Getting things done and avoiding having too many spanners thrown in the wheels all the way to the "ribbon-cutting ceremony" and the first employee engagement results that show movement in the right direction. (Move)[1]

---

1   These are the seven elements of the MYPRISM framework, co-authored by Rolf Pfeiffer and published by Ideas for Leaders Publishing, August 2023.

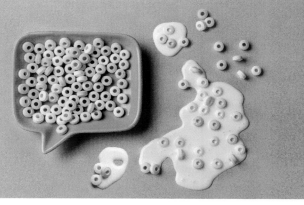

If we allowed ourselves to have honest conversations, we would get to functioning results much quicker.

If we allowed ourselves to have honest conversations, and to invest some time in the early stages of the development of such ideas, we would get to functioning results much quicker. If we were all prepared to be honest, to hear what we need to hear (vs. just hearing what we want to hear), to be respectful with all constituents involved, we would then get to effective decision-making, in pursuit of a well-stated objective, along an agreed and sensible timeline.

For those who agree that higher levels of sustainability of leader and employee roles are desirable, as they help to create higher levels of employee engagement (usually leading to better business results), here are some more ideas of what we can do to increase levels of sustainability:

By honestly speaking with and listening to one another we can create transformative insights.

- Youth – when speaking about the future of a business, or when creating ideas to develop the future of a business, it is critically important to also include the future (i.e. youth) in this conversation. Sounds easy and obvious, but it is not mainstream practice.
- Diversity – even though it might be demanding or painful at times, we are all well advised to speak with and listen to people who are different from us. Only that will allow us to broaden our perspective and see established things in a different light or see new things as they are relevant for the development of our organizations.
- Empathy, curiosity, and gratitude are great elements to underpin conversations especially with critics or opponents. By honestly speaking with and listening to one another we can create transformative insights.
- Pull vs Push – change is a lot easier if there is an attractive pull (i.e., towards motivation) rather than a punitive push (i.e., away-from motivation). This has been proven by, among others, Professor Richard Boyatzis in his work on the intentional change theory.

Hope – those who say that one of the key roles of leaders is to create hope are certainly right – hope is a key ingredient of successful change, whilst cynicism is one of the biggest enemies of and obstacles to change.

Make it Personal

And, if the opportunity arises, make it personal:

During a recent World Economic Forum conference, there was a panel of CEOs, each representing companies with more than 100,000 employees, on the broad topic of sustainability, and what was required of "big business" to make good on their promises. In the late evening before this panel was supposed to happen, the organizers were alerted to the fact that a highly visible leader of the "Fridays for Future" movement of young climate activists was going to be in the room. After some hectic back and forth between nine and eleven o'clock that night, it was decided to invite this person onto the panel.

The panellists were informed, additional briefings were offered, and the panel opened with everyone being supremely nervous about what would happen next. The activist waited for her turn to share opening remarks and, recognizing that everyone else on the panel was a member of her parents' generation, asked a simple question: "how do you convince your own children that your companies are embarking on the right course towards more sustainability?". Everyone in the room, and most certainly the organizers of the panel, held their breath. One after the other, all the panellists answered the question, revealing how important they felt the question was and how seriously they took the topic. They actually spoke of their own children, and how they (their children) were trying to hold them (the executives) to account. Much to the organizer's delight, everyone came away from this very rich conversation feeling that this had been one of the most impactful sessions during the entire multi-day conference. It was proof that under the right conditions, and with a degree of courage, even supposedly hard-nosed CEOs can have very human conversations with each other in public and are very aware of the role of their respective companies in creating more sustainable business. And whilst everyone can always do more, let's recognize what is being done today and take it as a good step in the right direction.

Permission

From this account, it became clear that C-Suite leaders who are willing to take societal concerns seriously and to put people first have far greater opportunities than those who do not. It takes the "tone from the top" to give permission to people at different levels in organizations to pursue ideas that can make businesses and their operations more sustainable – not just in terms of classical 'ecological' sustainability, but more importantly in terms of 'people' and 'financial' sustainability.

The importance, specifically of the topic of personal sustainability, has grown immensely since the beginning of the pandemic in early 2020. For those who can work

Most people find it difficult to "say no" and even more difficult to "do no".

from home, or from anywhere, the lines between time spent working and time spent away from working have blurred a lot more, putting an extra strain on many. The phenomenon of not being able to properly switch-off from work has become a lot more common. For those who want to make meaningful contributions through their work, no matter which company, industry, profession, or sector they operate in, this has become much harder to do and often exceeds the ability to adapt to new circumstances, and to leave behind old behaviours that are no longer suitable to changing situations.

Most people find it difficult to "say no" and even more difficult to "do no". In other words, asking for more resources, more budgets, more time has not been properly replaced by an honest conversation around what can be done and what cannot be done with the given time, energy, people, and budgets available. Not having the courage to have this conversation seems to be one of the biggest risks to personal sustainability. Accepting that people find themselves in an almost constant situation of 'overwhelm' effectively reduces everyone's ability to cope and seriously undermines any idea of self-efficacy.

It is easy to see how teams all passionately pulling in one direction can get a lot of things done, while passionately playing a game of tug-of-war consumes enormous amounts of energy without really allowing people to get anywhere.

Passion – Good and Bad

Today's organizations often communicate around passion. Passion for their products, for the contribution they can make to society, or, as a variation of passion, their obsession to improve their customers' lives. Passion can help enormously, as passionate people usually are in high-energy mode, which in turn facilitates getting things done. At the same time, passion can be a double-edged sword. When used wisely, it can invite collaboration and get others to enthusiastically join the bandwagon of an idea, when not used wisely it can effectively stop organizations from getting things done if opposing ideas are passionately being promoted, trying to convince others how they are superior and should therefore be pursued. It is easy to see how teams all passionately pulling in one direction can get a lot of things done, while passionately playing a game of tug-of-war consumes enormous amounts of energy without really allowing people to get anywhere.

Which leads me to the final question, as a repetition of the opening question: Do we all agree what 'higher levels of sustainability' look like? In my experience, this is a conversation that happens far too rarely. And the risk is that we all use the same word without ever trying to find out what we mean by it. Failure to have this conversation will make any progress a lot more difficult.

My wish, therefore, is for any team in any organization to start here. Have an honest conversation to define what 'higher levels of sustainability' really mean for you – what is visible and tangible in how people interact that makes the place more sustainable.

Rolf Pfeiffer *is co-managing director of Schwarz & Pfeiffer Executive Advisory Partners and a Fellow of the Institute of Coaching (IOC) at Harvard. He and his colleagues support senior executives and their teams internationally.*

References:

- *MYPRISM –* **www.kantologos.com**
- *Institute of Coaching Conference (Barcelona, 2022)* – **tinyurl.com/barcelona-reflections**

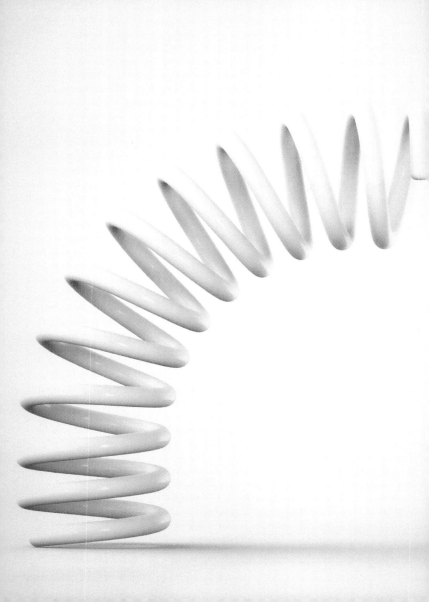

Julian Roberts

Promoting Team Resilience Through Authentic Leadership

A plethora of complexities, obstacles and shifting environments confronts organizations globally, often causing disruption and uncertainty, which can potentially impact their existence. Although perhaps now a cliché example, the recent pandemic does stand as an excellent precedent of the capability of organizations and employees to respond to challenges and uncertainty. A positive response became critically important: not just for navigating the crisis but also for creating a place to thrive which is sustainable and competitive for the future.

Although individual employee resilience reaps many benefits, the reality is that we work in teams.

By definition, resilience is "the process of adapting well in the face of adversity, trauma, tragedy, threats, or significant sources of stress". Studies show that resilient employees are not only better equipped to deal with challenges but also to navigate and overcome these events more successfully, always recognizing the positive meaning around negative experiences, enabling them to be more flexible, agile and perform better over time. Resilience is essential for teams and organizations to succeed.

Although individual employee resilience reaps many benefits, the reality is that we work in teams. By consciously boosting team resilience, teams will be better equipped for a crisis and thus perform better. However, contrary to the assumption that bringing a group of highly resilient people together will create a resilient team, even highly resilient people can suffer from issues of communication, leadership conflicts, challenges of accountability and different mental models in how they operate together. Individuals with high levels of resilience frequently exhibit a form of "toughness" that manifests in both their abilities and their psychological make-up. Occasionally, they may act without regard for the team, focusing solely on their individual concerns; this can have a negative effect on the team.

Considering the evident importance of team resilience to organizations, it is essential to understand and articulate the key components of resilience development. The existence of innovative cultures, collaboration, and creativity are all fundamental components to creating and developing resilient teams and organizations. With leadership highly influencing the presence of these components, it is thus vital to understand a leader's approach and style.

Authentic Leadership: What is it?

Given the unequivocal significance of leadership in creating team resilience, what style of leadership genuinely endorses resilience?

A key construct that is essential to success is authenticity: Becoming conscious of and accepting responsibility for one's own life experiences, as well as exhibiting and being true to oneself. Demonstrating authentic leadership requires self-awareness and self-control, which ultimately enables leaders to be more flexible and creative in their mental processes, allowing them to aid their staff in coping with hardship.

To understand what authentic leadership truly is, and how we can incorporate beneficial qualities into our leading style, let us briefly explore the "four dimensions" that constitute authentic leadership.

Possessing *self-awareness* is the first vital pillar of authenticity. Knowing who you are, what drives you, what your strengths are, and where you need to grow to be a

Balanced processing is the capacity to process information from those around you and make a pertinent decision

more effective leader, whilst also being conscious of your influence on others – these are all aspects of self-aware-ness and critical to becoming an authentic leader.

The second pillar is balanced processing, defined as "the capacity to process information from those around you and make a pertinent, sound judgement and rele-vant decision, ensuring you have elicited information from those around you". By exhibiting balanced process-ing, the authentic leader appears aware of each team member's feelings when making group decisions.

Next, with organizations' drive to deliver profit targets, many leaders will do anything to achieve this and appear to have a low priority for ethics and moral behaviour. Making sure that leaders adhere to their values and ideals in relation to the outside world while also upholding a standard of ethics, professionalism, and integrity is known as *having an internal moral perspective*.

And lastly, there is pressure for leaders to be *open and transparent*. Much of the reason for this transparency comes from corporate scandals, where confidence has been eroded for both employees and shareholders of the company, hence the need for openness and transparency. Authentic leaders will be true to their words, deeds, and principles, and it is essential that this is transparent to their followers. Additionally, relationship openness ensures that employees see their actual thoughts and emotions when appropriate, helping to embed and build trust.

How Does Authentic Leadership Promote Resilience?

While these four dimensions of authentic leadership evidence the "what" and "why" of such a leadership style, the "how" is perhaps more integral, especially with the increased realization of the value of developing team resilience.

Several aspects within an organization influence authentic leadership. Building follower efficacy is the first. This is done by the leader instilling confidence and trust in their team which results in their teams understanding their capabilities. Secondly, authentic leadership inspires optimism. High-hope individuals are those who consistently maintain an optimistic and proactive attitude, believing in their ability to surmount obstacles and achieve

High-hope individuals are those who consistently maintain an optimistic and proactive attitude, believing in their ability to surmount obstacles and achieve positive outcomes

positive outcomes. They have a remarkable capacity to overcome obstacles inherent to achieving their objectives. These obstacles can have a dual character, encouraging higher aspirations on the one hand and posing obstacles on the other. Regardless of the nature of the obstacle, these individuals place a high value on achieving their objectives, demonstrating exceptional adaptability in the face of change. In addition, they excel at cultivating interdependent relationships which are based on mutual support, collaboration, and shared goals. They have a commendable ability to maintain emotional equilibrium and composure even when confronted with demanding or challenging situations. This enables them to make logical decisions and respond effectively, as opposed to succumbing to excessive tension or negative emotions. Reports suggest that leaders with higher hope tended to have more profitable organizations, more fulfilled employees, and a lower staff turnover. Resilient organisations are established on the basis of a realistic assessment of the challenges present in their environment and a firm belief in their ability to effectively overcome these challenges. This duality between recognising obstacles and maintaining a positive outlook is the essence of resilience. Authentic leadership acts as a catalyst, fostering an environment where this mindset can flourish and ultimately leading to organisational success in spite of adversity.

My research examined the connection between authentic leadership and team resiliency. The study was conducted in 2022 as part of my thesis for my MSc in Psychology; 95 participants from 17 countries, working in teams of at least three members and reporting to the team's line manager, participated. Each participant completed two surveys, one on the manager's authentic leadership and the other on the team's resiliency. The study found a strong and significant correlation between authentic leadership and team resilience. It was found that authentic leadership positively predicts team resilience. Although each of the four dimensions of authentic leadership contributes to promoting team resilience, when examined in greater detail, self-awareness, and internal moral perspective, in particular, emerged as key predictors of team resilience.

The Power of Authentic Leadership: Promoting Resilience through Self-Awareness

As a leader develops greater self-awareness, they begin to see their advantages, disadvantages, and blind spots. This apparent awareness fosters team member trust and raises their standing among the group. Being self-aware as a leader enhances the significance of ongoing growth and development and encourages a culture of learning and development. A leader's self-awareness fosters an environment conducive to team learning, and team learning enables the team to analyse, comprehend, and adapt to the circumstances at hand, ultimately leading to team improvement. What is more, research shows that an open, accommodating, collaborative, and learning-focused work atmosphere helps employees develop resilience. In order to create a team that is highly focused on learning, leaders must create a culture of learning, promote a climate of openness and trust, and set an example for their team; it has been shown that leaders can influence group behaviour through exemplary behaviours. All of these actions are made possible by the leader's self-awareness.

Since self-awareness fosters this team learning environment, along with the fact that resilience is increased, the ability to navigate fresh new challenges requires a different way of thinking and mindset - this is developed and fostered from a learning-orientated environment.

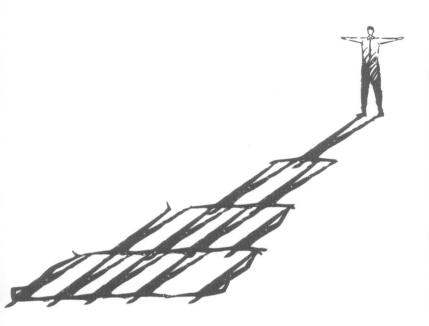

In order to create a team that is highly focused on learning, leaders must create a culture of learning,

Moreover, when a person or organization exhibits the capability to be adaptable, versatile, and resilient in the face of difficult circumstances, they are said to be flexible. This level of adaptability within the team setting gives the team members the chance to express their emotions without worrying about being punished, ultimately encouraging experimentation and inventiveness. Several models suggest that flexibility is key to effective leadership and the building of resilient teams. The "greatest leaders" don't come from a certain personality type; rather, effective leaders are able to adjust and alter their behaviour depending on the circumstances. Self-awareness and flexibility are related, with more self-aware leaders found to be more inclined to adapt their leadership style to the situation. Additionally, self-awareness of a leader predicts team flexibility, ultimately contributing to the team's capacity for resilience.

As a result of the self-awareness component of authentic leadership, the team's capacity for resilience is increased and an open and learning atmosphere is fostered, allowing team learning orientation and team flexibility to thrive.

The Power of Authentic Leadership: Promoting Resilience through Internal Moral Perspective

As the other key authentic leadership component that predicted resilience, internal moral perspective was found to be associated with task design and group norms, both of which form part of the enabling structure of a resilient team.

Internal moral perspective was also found to be a predictor of task design. Task design is all about giving team members complete autonomy over work processes and decisions regarding the entire piece of work, assuring constant feedback on the team's performance. Carefully crafted tasks provide the flexibility, autonomy, and resources that team members need to make decisions in difficult circumstances. In order for a task to have "motivating potential", it must align with the team's overall objective. For the team to consistently provide reliable outcomes, the team task must be relevant and in line with the overall goal, and each member must have the autonomy to make decisions on the work methods.

Task design also relates to a meaningful and purposeful piece of work: Work that is contributing to the bigger picture along with work that requires 'judgment calls' based on the values of the team and leader. It is essential for a leader to have an internalized moral perspective when making decisions and generating meaningful work in a team. This ensures that the leader aligns their values and beliefs with the reasoning and actions of the rest of the world according to a standard of professionalism and integrity. This inspires trust among the team because congruence creates trust and makes the connection between our inner world and outer activity very obvious.

If you want to boost the resilience of your teams, you should choose leaders who exhibit authentic leadership behaviours

Internal moral perspective was also found to be a predictor of group norms. To have group norms, individuals must adhere to clear, well-defined standards of behaviour and conduct, while keeping in mind the expectations that all group members share. A sense of purpose and belonging is essential for the team to have while dealing with challenging conditions, and having clear and explicit shared norms of behaviour and conduct is crucial. It is important that early on in the development of a team the basic group norms of member behaviour are established.

In conclusion, the internal moral perspective was found to be a predictor of task design and group norms; both of which are increased within a team if the leader is aligned with their internal moral beliefs and ensures they are exercised in the external setting. This aspect of authentic leadership cultivates awareness and explicitness of values, beliefs and purposeful leadership, which enables task design and group norms to flourish and therefore increase the ability of the team to be resilient.

Building Resilient Teams: A Pragmatic Approach for Leaders

Organizations are increasingly realizing the value of developing team resilience, to enable employees to weather the storm of shocks and challenges that they face either personally or within the organization. The study that I conducted[1] indicates the predictive value

---

1   https://www.julianrobertsconsulting.com/psychology-thesis

of authentic leadership on team resilience and demonstrates that team resilience is related to characteristics such as higher team performance, team learning, and positive emotions linked with individual resilience.

Leaders can foster a team climate characterized by a growth mindset, openness, and learning orientation by highlighting the importance of development, encouraging, emphasising, and rewarding various learning activities, as well as giving their direct reports the room to promote open discussion, experiment with novel ideas, learn from past mistakes, and find innovative solutions in the face of adversities.

Indirectly, the research suggests that if you want to boost the resilience of your teams, you should firstly choose leaders who exhibit authentic leadership behaviours. Next, a focus should be put on training and development initiatives aimed at boosting authentic leadership into practice, and finally to raise awareness of team resilience.

Julian Roberts is an executive leadership coach, committed to fostering resilience in both individuals and teams. His extensive background spans 20 years in the corporate sector, where he excelled in guiding and nurturing commercial and sales teams.

Andrew Dyckhoff

Energy Matters: Thriving in an uncertain world

We live in turbulent times. Just as organizations emerged from the impact of Covid-19 they entered a new period of uncertainty driven by world events and the consequent inflationary pressures. After two years of lockdown, organization energy levels were already depleted. The need to digitize, create new ways of working and manage disrupted supply chains to survive has resulted in huge project workloads on top of business-as-usual responsibilities.

This combination of uncertainty and long working hours has led to initiative fatigue and going forward we will have to 'do more with even less'. Organizations are grappling with new ways of (hybrid) working. All this adds up to a 'perfect storm'.

This combination of uncertainty and long working hours has led to initiative fatigue and going forward we will have to 'do more with even less'.

Business impact of organizational energy

Dame Carol Black, distinguished clinician and author of "Working for a Healthier Tomorrow", once said to me "You do realize that as a CEO you can do more for the health and wellbeing of people than I can as a clinician!"

Organizations with high levels of positive energy are resilient and consistently deliver great results. Highly energized employees are happier and more fulfilled. There is a clear win/win for business and society if we can create business environments that foster energy. In this article we share key insights into organization energy from research and practice and suggest practical ways to translate insight into action.

Insight No.1 - Organization energy drives performance

Intuitively we know that energy matters. The evidence supports this intuition. Leadership energy levels correlate with financial performance. Energy fuels organizations' success. Data from working with a major financial institution showed that high energy leaders were approximately 3 times more profitable than low energy leaders. Thus, the well-known formula "Strategy + Execution = Results" might better be cast as:

(Strategy + Execution) x Energy = Results

Insight No. 2 - Energy decreases over time

Every system in the universe loses energy. The second law of thermodynamics says that entropy always increases with time and organizations, their teams and their people are no exception. Rather like a hot air balloon, organizations need to be constantly re-energized to maintain their altitude and if they are to go higher the energy levels must be substantially increased.

Insight No. 3 - Leaders are the primary catalysts

The level of energy in the system is driven by the level of leadership energy. Systems naturally tend towards equilibrium and organizations are no exception. To maintain the system requires energy. If the energy inputs fall below the levels required for maintenance, the performance levels fall and potentially lead to failure.

Low energy environments typically manifest a strongly hierarchical approach to leadership in which the leaders seek to control people and outcomes.

To increase results, you need to increase the level of leadership energy, which in turn shifts the organization energy leading to higher levels of customer service and profitability.

Insight No. 4 - The difference energy makes

Levels of energy correlate with performance levels and systems consistently display symptoms associated with differing levels of energy. Low energy environments typically manifest a strongly hierarchical approach to leadership in which the leaders seek to control people and outcomes. High energy environments manifest an approach based on trusting people to perform in a collaborative environment. This is illustrated opposite:

As leaders we need to take a good hard look at our own organizations and ask ourselves whether we are manifesting the "symptom" in the top right of the chart.

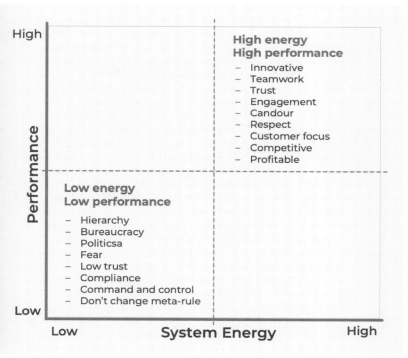

Insight No. 5 – There is an energy gap

We want our leaders to energize us.

Zenger Folkman has researched the key attributes of leaders that deliver exceptional business results. As part of their research, they sought to understand which leadership traits are most valued by employees. In two hundred and fifty thousand 360-degree surveys Zenger Folkman

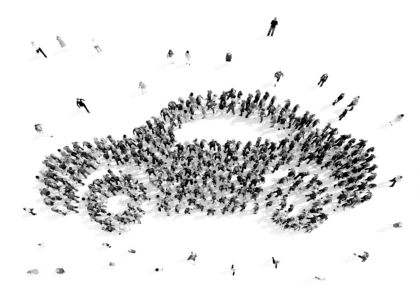

Where we fall short is in creating the fuel that drives the vehicle: organization energy.

asked 1.6 million raters to state what is most important for their boss to have, to be successful in their role.

The standout Number 1 ranked competency was "Inspires and Motivates to high levels of effort and performance". Two of the three items used to measure this relate to the leader's capacity to energize others.

When we look at the results in the global database of 130,000 leaders, it would be reasonable to anticipate that scores for "Inspires and Motivates" should benchmark somewhere in the middle of the 19, on the basis that some leaders will score highly and some not. The sad reality is that it comes out at the bottom of the rankings. Leaders are generally least capable in inspiring, motivating and so energizing their people

This speaks to an energy gap across our organizations.

Organization as a "vehicle"

Using the metaphor of organizations as a vehicle, the results from the Zenger Folkman research show that we are great at building the vehicle and demonstrate the associated leadership traits.

Vehicle building activities include setting the strategy, building the product, hiring people, setting and driving KPIs. This capacity is reflected in high scores across the global database for technical and professional expertise, effort and driving for results.

Where we fall short is in creating the fuel that drives the vehicle: organization energy.

Bridging the energy gap

Leaders are the catalysts. As a mentor once taught me, as the leader it is "always all my fault". This reflects the

The starting point is to recognize that leadership is about our followers and that we need to create the conditions in which they will do great work.

power that we have as leaders to influence the environments we create for our people. The starting point is to recognize that leadership is about our followers and that we need to create the conditions in which they will do great work. Recognition leads us to focus on how we create roles and delegate tasks in such a way that our people are energized.

Leadership 'levers' for success.

The Zenger Folkman research has identified the two most powerful leadership competencies (levers) as "Drives for Results" and "Inspires and Motivates Others to High Levels of Effort and Performance". These are displayed by exceptional leaders, defined as those who deliver results in the top 10% of results in their industry. To understand what this means in practice it is helpful to look at the measures for each of the levers:

The measures for Drives for Results are:
- Does everything possible to achieve goals
- Achieves the agreed goals within the time allotted
- Follows through on objectives to ensure successful completion

The measures for Inspires and Motivates are:
- Energizes people to achieve exceptional results
- Inspires others to high levels of effort and performance
- Brings to the group a high level of energy and enthusiasm

Organizations value leaders by the results they deliver. We promote leaders who give their all and follow through on the "vehicle building" traits, but we rarely ask ourselves what the leader's impact on energy levels might be.

The power of "and"

When we look at the data the strongest results are created when both "Drives for results" and "Inspires and motivates" are deployed. Statistically, if a leader has only one part and not the other at a top quartile level, the chances of delivering top decile results are approximately 12%. However, when the two are combined the chance is not 24%, but 74%!

Given the tendency for most organizations to focus on the vehicle building levers such as driving for results, it is likely that our organization's results, however good, are sub-optimal. Focusing on creating more energy to fuel the vehicle we can create a positive shift not only in the results of the business but the employee experience at work, which in turn positively impacts the health and well-being of our people.

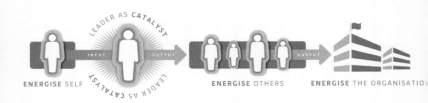

Personal:
- Own Energy – Mental, Physical, Spiritual, Emotional
- Capability and Suitability

Interpersonal:
- Energizes others (authentic leadership)
- Builds Capability – Individual, Team, Organisation

Systemic:
- Sees patterns and connections
- Collaborator for longer term impact

Generating system energy – in practice

To be effective in maintaining and increasing the organization energy, leaders need to pay attention to three areas: personal energy, interpersonal energy and systemic energy.

The pressures of work and demands of home life often mean that personal care suffers.

1.   Personal – energize self

Leaders need to take care of their own energy, mental, physical, spiritual, emotional. In turbulent times this can be difficult to do. The pressures of work and demands of home life often mean that personal care suffers. Whilst it is possible to survive in the short- and medium-term, extended periods of stress lead to a long-term decline in performance.

Post-Covid, organizations have become much better at paying attention to the wellbeing of their people. There is a wide range of help available...the secret is to take action to avail yourself of the help.

Energy is also about capacity and capability. Focusing on playing to strengths and continuing to invest in learning to develop new skills, disciplines and habits creates new energy to input into the system.

Creating clear and compelling personal goals and ensuring these are aligned with their role in the organization underpins the capacity to energize the organization.

2.   Interpersonal – energize others

Since leaders are the primary catalysts in determining the level of organization energy, they need to be able to inspire and motivate and energize the people they lead in an authentic way. This means the leader needs to invest in understanding and being able to articulate what makes them special, their "superpowers". Psychometric instruments are helpful in both revealing what these are and giving a language for expressing them in words that are both accurate and accessible to others.

When deployed across a team, it is possible to create a shared language that supports effective collaboration. In our experience it is rare that leaders and teams take the time to deeply understand each other's motivations and sources of energy. If we imagine members of a team as cogs that mesh with one another, a lack of understanding means the cogs rattle against each other. Losing energy in the process. By investing in creating genuine understanding and mutual appreciation, team interactions become more efficient and effective, leading to better decisions made more quickly.

Our solution is to use data to pinpoint the strengths of a leader. We start by calibrating the leader's current capability. The Strengths Unleashed Triangulation® approach uses three different lenses to bring the leader into clear focus:

We assess:

- what drives them
- what they are thinking
- where they fit

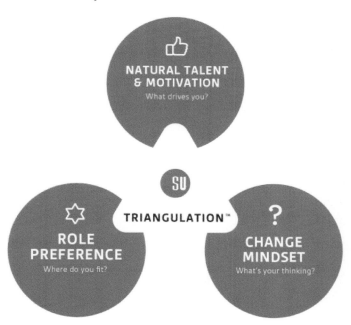

What drives you?

Energy and drive come from the use of our natural talents in pursuit of our goals. Leaders who know what drives them remain energized no matter what the challenge.

Mapping the leader's natural talent set and finding out what motivates them to come to work helps them identify the top 10 strengths they should play to and pinpoint the source of their energy and drive.

What are you thinking?

The leader's mindset is mission critical.

Everyone has embedded, unconscious patterns of thinking that show up in their behaviours. When seeking to make things happen, these patterns are at play. If aligned with the leader's energetic strengths – and with the needs of the business – great things happen. Misalignment frequently leads to underperformance and a failure to create the desired impact.

We use the GC Index, a powerful organimetric instrument, to surface the leader's unconscious thinking and assess their ability to drive the right kind of organizational impact, whether through innovation, transformation, or execution.

Where do you fit?

There is a persistent myth that strong leadership means being good at everything.

The data shows that great leaders are exceptional in a few areas and know how to leverage these strengths to deliver results. This translates into a strong preference for a particular role in the organization or a certain part of the business lifecycle.

Leaders who energize others also recognize the importance of developing capability in individuals, teams, and the wider organization.

By mapping leaders' preferences across possible roles in different stages of the business cycle we identify where they perform at their best and then help them to maximize their contribution within their preferred role.

Developing others

Leaders who energize others also recognize the importance of developing capability in individuals, teams, and the wider organization. Leaders who focus on making their people more successful command loyalty and foster high levels of discretionary effort.

Finding the sweet spot

Research from Zenger Folkman shows that there is a sweet spot for individuals, teams, and organizations where competence, energy and a compelling goal intersect. It is therefore vital that others also have individual and collective goals that align with their role in the organization.

Whilst it is common to assess individual leaders' impact through assessment, such as 360s, organizations do not often look at the whole system impact of the leadership.

3. Systemic – energize the organization

The desired result of leaders as catalysts is an energized and capable organization, aligned behind a shared ambition, delivering results today, whilst transforming for the future.

Leaders therefore need to measure the impact they are having on the organization. Whilst it is common to assess individual leaders' impact through assessment, such as 360s, organizations do not often look at the whole system impact of the leadership.

At the system level, leaders need to ensure that the vision, purpose, and mission of the organization is both compelling (energizing) and fit for purpose in volatile and rapidly changing circumstances. They also need to ensure that resources and effort are directed at both delivering results today and simultaneously re-inventing the organization to remain competitive and meet their customers' evolving needs.

A powerful way to effect systemic change

Our partner Quanta Consulting has developed a distinctive and highly effective approach to change called 'Energy Fractals.' A fractal is an infinitely complex pattern that is self-similar across different scales consisting of simple building blocks which, with repetition, evolve into complex systems.

An energy fractal is a new behaviour that, when consistently repeated, has a powerful impact on the system. To take an example from daily life, if you want to get fit the fractal might be exercise 3x per week. The first order impact is improved fitness. The second order impact goes far beyond this. See illustration below:

1st Order Impact

- Improved Fitness

2nd Order impact

- Energy Levels?
- Stress management?
- Employee relationships?
- Customer service?
- Profitability?

Experience shows that simple behavioural shifts specifically designed to address issues diagnosed in the organization energy survey have powerful positive effects. If we take, for example, communication (an area that frequently requires attention) an energy fractal to address this might look like this:

A simple habit (have a conversation with each team member once a week) has the capacity to deliver multiple benefits at the personal, interpersonal, and the systemic level.

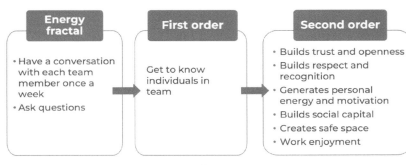

Closing reflections

Organizations that focus on energy as well as driving for results are more likely to thrive in turbulent times. Leaders who inspire and motivate their teams re-energize them. Employees who are energized in pursuit of a compelling goal rarely look outside the organization and bring elevated levels of discretionary effort to their work, which leads to higher levels of profitability. The focus on energy as the fuel that propels the organization is a powerful unifying idea that focuses on the "so what" of leadership, in delivering exceptional performance. As we continue to face new challenges, understanding and acting on the insight that leaders have the capacity to catalyze new levels of energy increases the chance that we will not only survive, but thrive in the emerging new world.

Andrew Dyckhoff is the Founder and CEO of Strengths Unleashed. An inspiring and passionate speaker, Andrew has an extraordinary network of leaders who share his values of generosity, curiosity and life-long learning. His focus is on organisational energy and helping businesses, and their people, achieve more with what they have.

Marilyn Mehlmann

Ancient Wisdom, Modern Leadership

The synthetical leader

t started with a question. I was, yet again, bewailing the fact that we teach, and teach, and teach analysis in our schools and universities, whereas in today's world - specifically, with complex issues like sustainable development to deal with - we need synthesis skills at least as much, if not more. And we don't teach synthesis.

"So how would you teach synthesis?" was the question. A good one. A colleague and I debated, searched, thought... and settled on a document that was several thousand years old, from the Dead Sea Scrolls. In the scrolls a tribe or sect called the Essenes documented, among many other things, some simple rules for living

In the scrolls a tribe or sect called the Essenes documented, among many other things, some simple rules for living a good life.

a good life. And we saw how we could use those rules to benefit leaders wanting to learn how to synthesize better: how to make better decisions in situations of rapid change and complex challenges.

Why synthesis is important

Synthesis is about pattern recognition and sensemaking. Analysis is important when it comes to collecting data - as long as the reasons for collecting it are clear, and clearly relevant.

But how do we know that? How can we be sure that we have collected all the most relevant data? With an analytical approach it is possible to include 'what-if' questions about trends, whether by extrapolation or exaggeration; but what about the disrupters, trend-breakers, 'black swans'?

> *Not everything that counts can be counted. And not everything that can be counted, counts.*
> – William Bruce Cameron (Sociologist)

And not least: what about people's reactions to what happens?

The one thing we know for certain about people is that they will surprise us. – anonymous psychologist

And then. How to make sense of the data? This is a universal stumbling block encountered as frequently in academia as in business. Unless the data is really unequivocal, there is a risk that the original idea or hypothesis, used to design the data collection, is simply reformulated as the conclusion. See, the data confirmed what we suspected all along!

Sensemaking, the province of synthesis rather than analysis, relies heavily on the skill of listening, in the broadest possible sense. The listening first makes it possible to improve data collection, and then to enable better sensemaking.

Key questions: Who do we listen to? When? And how do we listen?

The Dead Sea keys to synthesis

From the above, it is clear that successful synthesis builds on successful relationships. If we listen, but people only tell us what they think we want to hear and not what they truly feel or think, then we might as well not bother.

This is where the Essenes come in. There are nine Essene guidelines: seven of them related to relationships and sensemaking, neatly bookended by two related to peace of mind.

A mindset for outstanding leadership

The bookends are tranquillity and serenity.

Tranquillity: *I choose inner peace, regardless of the circumstances. The goal is to practise peace which radiates out into relationships.*

Serenity: *My inner peace is strong even when put to hard tests. I no longer need to choose tranquillity.*

These two bookends express something central to good leadership: the ability to observe without judging. Being non-judgmental is not the same as being uncritical. Compare the following two sentences:

'Last week the number of product returns was nearly 100% above average. Has a reason for this been identified?'

Really listening, which means also hearing what is said and what is left unsaid, without distractions, without judgement or other filters.

'The number of product returns is entirely unacceptable! Who is responsible for the increase?'

Inspired by the Essenes, we can add one more of their guidelines, 'Joy in mistakes', to describe a mindset: outstanding leadership characterized by a mindset of tranquil service and continuous learning.

Tranquillity. *I choose inner peace, regardless of the circumstances. My goal is to practise peace which radiates out into relationships.*

Joy in mistakes. *I strive to understand my own mistakes, joyfully, in order to learn from them.*

Serenity. *My inner peace is strong even when put to hard tests. I no longer need to choose tranquillity.*

Using our senses

Probably the single most important skill that a leader can cultivate is that of listening. Really listening, which means also hearing what is said and what is left unsaid, without distractions, without judgement or other filters. Through such focused listening, much information and wisdom can be gathered that is not accessible to conventional data collection. Three more Essene guidelines help with this.

> **The supporter.** *I strive to understand your true needs and to meet them, if this is practical without causing harm to others or myself. I treat my own needs with the same respect.*
>
> **The 'good eye'.** *I choose to see and relate to the positive in you, in others, and in myself.*
>
> **Holistic view, stakeholder perspective.** *We may see things differently. I respect your views and perspective without having to renounce my own. There are many paths to the same destination.*

These three tenets are useful not only for knowledge-gathering but also, not coincidentally, for building outstanding relationships. They also point to a journey of self-discovery. I listen to my own inner wisdom in order to identify my own needs, to recognize the positive in myself, to craft my own perspective and values.

This kind of listening, Deep Listening to oneself as well as to others, is a skill that can be taught, easy to learn though hard to perfect. To paraphrase, "Minutes to learn, a lifetime to master". Practising Deep Listening is an excellent source of material for 'Joy in mistakes'!

Sensing
Parking

An important element of deep listening is the ability to 'park' all the things that get in the way. When listening 'normally', we tend to filter everything we hear through a mesh of beliefs, values, knowledge, feelings, experience - including the immediate experience of the environment, with its sounds, colours, aromas, comfort or discomfort.

It comes as a surprise to many that our beliefs, thoughts and feelings can be safely parked until needed. We do not have to allow them to drive us endlessly round and round the same circuit.

Why should we want to park?

Well, just take a look at feelings. Emotions, like money and many other things in life, are magnificent servants and tyrannical masters. My feelings tell me that something is going on, and can help me understand and empathize with other people. They can also give me energy – or steal it.

Emotions make excellent servants, but tyrannical masters.
– John Seymour

Any situation can trigger feelings, positive or negative. They come in waves: first an emotional response to the actual situation, then a wave of fossil feelings ("This has happened to me before"), then often feelings about the feelings ("Darn, now I got upset again, why do I do that?").

Deep Listening is both new, and very old. It is about hearing the other (or yourself) without the kind of censorship exercised by experience, expectations and preconceived opinions.

It is not only our feelings that can block deep listening. There is a whole chorus of voices inside us clamouring for attention. For instance, our history ('Something JUST like that happened to me, once'), our situation ('Is it today I'm supposed to pick the kids up from football?'), our knowledge ('No that can't be right'), our beliefs and values ('Not sure I like where this is going'), or just our surroundings ('I wonder if there's any coffee left?').

Park them all. It doesn't mean they are irrelevant, just that this is not the time.

Deep Listening
It's easy to listen – we do it all the time!
We listen – but how do we listen? The quality of our listening has a great impact on the quality of our relationships, and thus of our meetings, whether formal or informal.

> *When I deep-listen I don't just hear what they say,*
> *I hear what they mean.*
> – Hunter-gatherer in Arctic Sweden

Deep Listening is both new, and very old. It is about hearing the other (or yourself) without the kind of censorship exercised by experience, expectations and preconceived opinions.

When listening to another person, the first rule is to 'BE silence': to quieten or park your own inner dialogue in order to pay full attention to the speaker. By extension this also means being silent, most of the time. The originator of Deep Listening, Warren Ziegler, found that the only good reason for a listener to speak is when they have a 'compelling question' that needs clarification in order for them to understand.

The second rule is perhaps counterintuitive: no eye contact. In fact we recommend sitting (or walking) such that you avoid seeing each other. When you give the listener no feedback of any kind (not even a smile!), there is a better chance that they will stop trying to please you, and say what they really need to say.

Listening to yourself is a bit like interviewing yourself: you start by formulating the question. For example, "How do I really feel about the conflict between A and B? Do I feel able to trust either of them?"

You are, in fact, interrogating your intuition, or tacit knowledge. We all know that we have it. We talk, for instance, about 'sleeping on' a question.

We all know that we know much more than we know we know.
– Warren Ziegler

Once the question is clear, the first step is the same as when listening to another person: quieten your own inner dialogue, including parking all your knowledge and beliefs, ask the question - and listen.

Whose voice?

So then new questions arise: when I listen to myself, who am I listening to? If this is meant to access the voice of my intuition: how do I know that is what I am hearing, and not just my hopes - or fears?

Ziegler gave some hints. The voice of your intuition, or deeper wisdom, is never judgmental, he said. So if you see or hear something telling you how stupid or bad you are, stay with the question, because you are not there yet. The same goes for positive judgments. Maybe you are indeed a wonderful person, leader, parent... that is fine, but keep listening.

He also said that the voice is never aggressive. I would add: it is never just repeating what you have been saying/thinking to yourself for weeks or months. There is an element of novelty - and often, humour.

Does it always work? No. For most people it takes some practice - not least the 'parking'. And occasionally that inner voice seems to have nothing to say. But it is always worth asking the question!

Speak, or remain silent?

When Deep Listening to another person, the general principle is to remain silent. But there can be exceptions, in particular for 'compelling questions'.

It may also happen that the speaker asks you to say something. Treat it as an invitation: you are not obliged to say anything. In many cases it can be best to respond with 'Please say more - I'm listening.' If you nonetheless feel you would like to say something, have a quick check against the Essene principles. Do I want to say this in order to help them clarify their needs (The supporter),

The only good reason for a listener to speak is when they have a 'compelling question' that needs clarification in order for them to understand.

show their best qualities (The good eye), or clarify where they stand in a question with multiple stakeholders? Or do I perhaps rather want to say this for my own benefit?

The compelling question

Sometimes when listening we come up against a comprehension barrier. Did they mean this, or that? Such questions can be difficult to park, because they can make it difficult to understand what is said afterwards. So, respectfully, we can interrupt to ask.

The 'I-message'

When speaking to another person or group - whether you are in Deep Listening mode or not - it is always useful to start with an 'I-message'. Indeed, most communications are improved when they start with 'I' rather than 'you'.

For instance, "I'm having difficulty reconciling what you say about xxx and what you say about yyy – can you explain?" is more helpful than: "You're contradicting yourself, it doesn't make sense!"

Marshall Rosenburg, author of Non-Violent Communication, called this 'giraffe language': being willing to stick your neck out.

Sense-making

The continuous process of listening enables the synthetical leader to discern perspectives, risks and opportunities that were not part of the original question, gaining a broader, more nuanced knowledge base.

Now we can add the last of the Essenes' guidelines, 'Fairness for all': a principle that is enshrined in the Sustainable Development Goals but not yet well defined or applied. This joins the 'Holistic view, stakeholder perspective' as a major tool for sense-making - naturally, together with 'Joy in mistakes'!

Holistic view, stakeholder perspective. *We see things differently. I respect your views and perspective without having to renounce my own. There are many paths to the same destination.*

Fairness for all. *My goal is to work for what is fairest for all, in any situation.*

Joy in mistakes. *I strive to understand my own mistakes, joyfully, in order to learn from them.*

Culture at work

This is about you, the leader. But not only about you.

Or, it is about your ability to develop a working culture that permits everyone to grow into this space of right relationship and discernment: to create space for genuine co-creation of new insights and opportunities. It starts, but does not stop, with your own ability to deep-listen.

Meetings matter

It is easy to slip into habitual ways of organizing meetings. There are however alternatives that promote the kind of listening recommended by the Essenes: ways that, to begin with, engage all participants in setting the agenda. Several are documented in the online Facilitating Transformation Toolbox[1]

Transparency matters

If you listen, and consult, and listen some more; and then simply announce your decision, with no hint of what

---

1 See in particular Fleck's Synergy method – hostingtransformation.eu/toolbox/

influenced you, there may be some backlash. It does not mean that everything needs to be explained at every stage, but that you share enough of your decision-making process to engender trust in whoever is affected: employees, customers, civil society...

Ethics, or good sense?

It is easy to frame the Essenes' guidance as 'good ethics'. And, there is more to it than that. There is that question of engendering trust, which has been shown to be highly operational:

"When trust is instilled in an organization, tasks get accomplished with less difficulty because people are more likely to collaborate and communicate with each other in productive ways. As a result, outcomes tend to be more successful," writes Abbey Lewis at Harvard Business Publishing, who continues:

"According to a study in Harvard Business Review, people at high-trust companies report 74% less stress, 106% more energy at work, 50% higher productivity, 13% fewer sick days, 76% more engagement, 29% more satisfaction with their lives, and 40% less burnout than people at low-trust companies."

Trust the ancient wisdom of the Essenes. And yourself.

Marilyn Mehlmann is the co-founder of Legacy17, and is focused on 'people skills' for sustainable development. She combines pychosynthesis, empowerment and action research to co-create methods and tools for personal and professional development.
www.legacy17.org

The Essenes were the third principal sect of Jews who lived at the time of Christ in Palestine, probably on the shores of the Dead Sea. They were ascetics who were devoted to healing.

The Essenes were the third principal sect of Jews who lived at the time of Christ in Palestine, probably on the shores of the Dead Sea. They were ascetics who were devoted to healing. There is some evidence they were connected with the Therapeuts, another sect of Jewish healers of the same period, who lived near Alexandria.

They were small in number, probably only a few thousand, and according to some, the Virgin Mary was an Essene and Jesus was with the Essenes during his 40 days in the wilderness.

These explanations to their Nine Principles were formulated by the author with Guy Pettitt, alongside the work of Edith Stauffer.

The Essene Gospel of Peace is an ancient manuscript found in the Vatican Library (which most improbably includes instructions for colonic irrigation) and was translated by Edmond Szekely, who is widely regarded as the leading modern interpreter of the Essenes's writings.

Principle	Opposite, or step on the way
Rukha Tranquillity. I choose inner peace, regardless of the circumstances. My goal is to practice peace which radiates out into relationships.	*Weather-vane, or victim of circumstances.*
Makikh The supporter. I strive to understand your true needs and to meet them, if practical without causing harm to others or myself. I treat my own needs with the same respect.	*Your needs do not interest me. Or, I know what you need and will give it to you, whether you want it or not.*
Abilii Joy in mistakes. I strive to understand my own mistakes, joyfully, in order to learn from them, and to re-vision the preferred behaviour instantly.	*One of us is right and the other is wrong. It's bad to be wrong.*
Kenoota Fairness for all. My goal is to work for what is fairest for all, in any situation.	*Revenge. Justice.*
Khooba The 'good eye'. I choose to see and relate to the positive in you, in others, and in myself. Unconditional positive regard.	*You're hardly perfect (and I don't think much of myself either).*

Principle	Opposite, or step on the way
Dadcean libhoun Holistic view, stakeholder perspective. We see things differently. I respect your views and perspective without having to renounce my own. There are many paths to the same destination.	*If you were as well informed and intelligent as I (and as benevolent), you would agree with me. Did I not express myself sufficiently clearly?*
Abdey shlama The peacemaker. I make no demands that you should change. I am open to your potential and my own.	*I know how you should be, for your own good. (And I can help you.)*
Rakhma Unconditional love. Through practice of abdey shlama, the god within me salutes the god within you.	*I love you so long as you do what I want, or, I expect you to do what I want because I love you.*
Serenity My unconditional love is strong even when put to hard tests. I no longer need to choose rukha.	

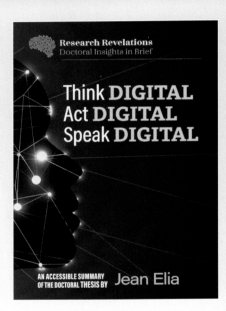

IDEAS FOR LEADERS

Academic research in accessible and engaging bite-sized chunks

IDEA #834

CORPORATE PURPOSE INSPIRES EMPLOYEE SUSTAINABILITY BEHAVIOURS

KEY CONCEPT

Employee perception of their company's purpose is a key driver of their sustainability behaviours at work, in part because corporate purpose increases psychological ownership of sustainability. This psychological ownership is even more intense for employees who believe strongly in the importance of being moral—and who have the autonomy to make sustainability decisions.

IDEA SUMMARY

The business world has increasingly accepted the concept of a corporate purpose that extends beyond profit and shareholder value. More and more companies recognize that their core purpose is to benefit all stakeholders, including customers, employees, and suppliers, as well as their communities and society at large.

Sustainability is a key element in a company's commitment to community and society. New research explains why working for a purpose-driven company inspires employees to engage in sustainability behaviours.

Employee sustainability behaviours can be ethically complex: to "do the right thing," employees must take into consideration different and sometimes conflicting stakeholder interests—for example, how to best benefit society by helping the environment but without hurting the company's economic interests.

In this situation, rules and regulations or universally accepted moral codes (e.g., "thou shalt not steal") are too narrow. To guide employees, companies need to frame the ethical issues involved in sustainability in a broader, more expansive manner.

Corporate purpose provides employees with this more expansive ethical guiding frame. The reason: while rules and regulations tell employee what right or wrong, corporate purpose inspires employees to take psychological ownership of sustainability.

Working for a purpose-driven company gives employees the sense that they are good, ethical people (self-identity), and the sense that they belong to a group that is working together for the greater good (belongingness). Self-identity and belongness are two of the basic human needs that sparks psychological ownership.

In the study, the researchers surveyed approximately 350 employees of the Indian subsidiary of a global manufacturer of heavy machinery. Analysis of the survey results confirmed the significant effect of corporate purpose on sustainability ownership, and the ensuing impact of sustainability ownership on sustainability behaviours.

The researchers also conducted a laboratory experiment that divided participants into two groups. The first group was asked to imagine that they worked for a fictional company with the stated purpose of "maximizing shareholder value." This purpose, the participants were told, "guided all of the company's policies and procedures, from procurement to marketing to packaging."

The second group imagined that they worked for a fictional company with a stated purpose of "nourishing families so they can flourish and thrive"—a purpose that, as with the first group "guided all of the company's policies and procedures, from procurement to marketing to packaging."

The respondents working for the "nourishing family" company expressed significantly greater ownership of sustainability and were significantly more likely to engage in a list of sustainability behaviours.

Two further studies, both surveys of actual employees, revealed two additional factors that reinforced the link between corporate purpose and employee sustainability behaviours.

The first survey of 241 employees of a German construction company showed that the greater the autonomy granted to employees for decisions related to sustainability, the greater the ownership felt by employees toward sustainability.

The second survey of more than 1000 employees from a variety of industries showed that sustainability autonomy had a greater impact on sustainability ownership the more individuals considered being a moral person (e.g., being caring, compassionate, fair, generous, hardworking, and honest) to be important.

The breadth of this last survey also confirmed the wide application of the link between corporate purpose and sustainability behaviours.

BUSINESS APPLICATION

The implications for managers and leaders are clear:

- Defining a corporate purpose that goes beyond share-holder value is a necessary first step to encouraging sustainability behaviours.
- To reinforce the impact of corporate purpose on sustainability behaviours, leaders should allow as much autonomy in sustainability decisions and actions as possible—not only at the employee-level, but also at the business unit or geographical location level since sustainability is often context-specific. For example, different locations may have different environmental issues; local units are thus better positioned than central headquarters to understand which actions benefit the environment and social issues most in their locations.
- Companies may want to make a special effort to "prime" their employees morally—giving them moral nudges through signages, webcasts, or sustainability ambassadors, for example—to further ensure the success of the company's sustainability efforts.

Access this and more *Ideas at* **ideasforleaders.com**

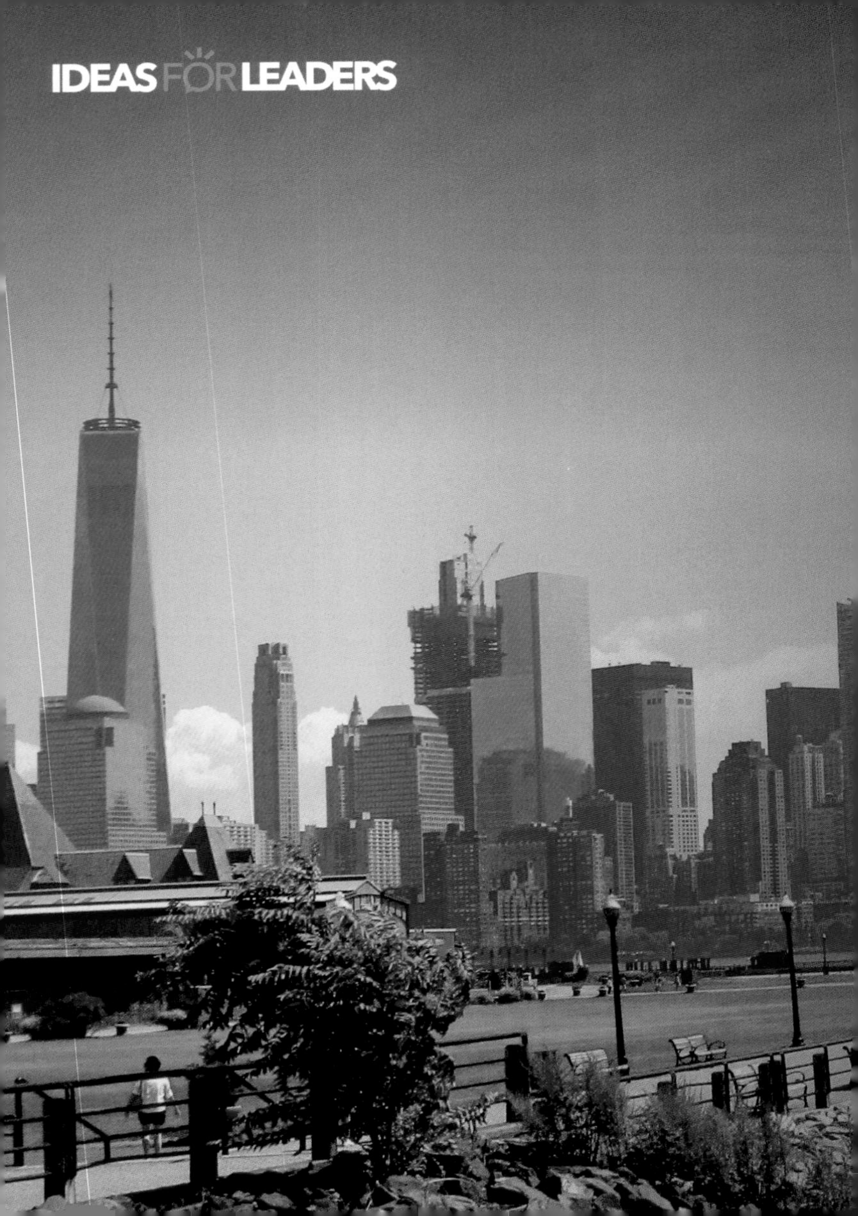
IDEAS FOR LEADERS

CSR BENEFITS TO SOCIETY FROM PRIVATE COMPANIES ARE GREATER THAN FROM PUBLIC COMPANIES

KEY CONCEPT

Does Corporate Social Responsibility (CSR) benefit society? A new study based on exhaustive data reveals that while private company CSR commitments do benefit society, public company do not perform as well.

IDEA SUMMARY

'Greenwashing' is a new term that describes the actions of companies whose corporate social responsibility (CSR) activities prove to be more window-dressing than action. Two Michigan Ross professors, Jun Li and Di (Andrew) Wu used a set of databases as proxies to answer a complex and important question: Does corporate social responsibility really benefit society?

The answer is not easy to uncover. Corporate social responsibility is a broad, multidimensional term that encompasses activities in environmental, society and governance (ESG) domains.

To develop a rigorous evidence-based answer, the researchers first identified companies that had signed on to the United Nations Global Compact, the world's largest CSR initiative, with more than 20,000 worldwide participants, including nearly 6,500 companies. In addition to the breadth of participation, another advantage of using the UNGC as the indicator of social responsibility is that participating companies are monitored by the UNGC (as opposed to other initiatives in which the companies self-report their activities).

The next step was identifying each company's impact

on society — a mammoth job that would not be possible without the unique RepRisk database. Monitoring more than 80,000 media, regulatory and business documents in 15 languages, RepRisk, a sustainability consultancy, screens public and private companies on a daily basis for negative ESG incidents, which can range from environmental damage incidents to social issues, such as labour relations conflict, to governance issues, such as executive compensation.

To answer the question at the heart of the research — does CSR benefit society? — Li and Wu analysed the negative ESG incidents for companies before and after they joined the Global Compact.

The results were striking. For private companies, the rate of negative ESG incidents decreased an average of 6.3% after they signed on to the UNGC. For public companies, however, there was no significant decrease in negative ESG incidents, and in fact in some cases, the data showed an increase in such incidents after the company had committed itself to corporate social responsibility.

A closer look reveals the reason for the disparity between the public and private company results: conflicts of interest between shareholders and other stakeholders. The owners of a private company have some flexibility in terms of trade-offs between doing good and doing well. They may be willing launch an initiative that may not be good for the bottom line but is good for society.

In public companies, this flexibility all but disappears. In blunt terms, if a CSR initiative or program is great for society but not so great for the company's shareholders, the needs of the shareholders are probably going to take priority.

On the other hand, if a CSR initiative is good for both stakeholders and shareholders, the initiative has a greater chance of being implemented. Thus, in areas of tax evasion, excessive CEO compensation or the wasting of resources, for example, the level of conflict (or conflict intensity) between the needs and desires of stakeholders and shareholder is low — i.e., everyone benefits if these problems are resolved. As a result, a commitment to the principles of the UNGC leads to decreases in incidents related to these areas.

In contrast, with issues related to collective bargaining situations, supply chains, or controversial products, for example, the conflict intensity is high— shareholders have different needs and wants than other stakeholders. As a result, even after public companies commit to CSR, there is no decrease in negative incidents related to these issues.

The research did reveal one interesting caveat to this general rule: public companies with consumer-facing products and services will follow up a commitment to CSR with a decrease in negative ESG incidents. The reason is clear: While B-to-B companies operate beyond the view (and interest) of the general public, consumers pay attention to the activities of compa-

nies such as retail chains or consumer product manufacturers. Just ask Nike. Thus, consumers will punish
any egregious failure to follow through with a stated
commitment to improving societal problems.

This consumer vigilance also explains why companies
downstream in the supply chain — thus closer to the
end consumer — are more likely to meet their CSR
commitments than upstream companies..

BUSINESS APPLICATION

Does corporate social responsibility help society? This
answer according to this research: depends on the
ownership type. The researchers reveal not only the
discrepancy between public and private companies
in CSR but also the economic explanation for this
discrepancy. Leaders of upstream or B-to-B companies who want to make a societal difference must be
prepared to confront this economic pressure, or watch
their companies fail to 'walk the talk' on CSR.

REFERENCES
Does Corporate Social Responsibility Benefit Society. Jun Li & Di
(Andrew) Wu. Ross School of Business Working Paper, No. 1335
(February 2017).

Access this and *more Ideas at* **ideasforleaders.com**

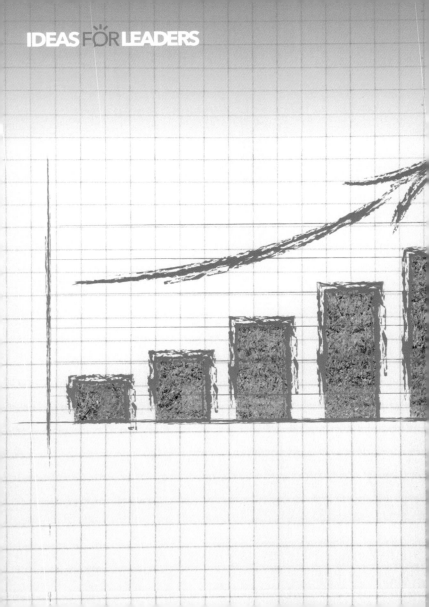

SUSTAINABILITY-DRIVEN HYBRID COMPANIES CHALLENGE BUSINESS DOGMA

KEY CONCEPT

The corporate world has embraced sustainability, but without challenging the basic rules of competition and economic success. Hybrid companies that blur the lines between business and societal/environmental missions prove that these rules can, and should, be challenged.

IDEA SUMMARY

Corporate sustainability has become mainstream. Few companies would argue today – as they argued in the past – that the only responsibility companies have to society is to make a profit. Today, corporations proudly describe their social responsibility initiatives.

Nardia Haigh of the School of Business at University of Massachusetts, Boston and Andrew Hoffman of the University of Michigan's Ross School of Business argue, however, that the concept of corporate sustainability has been diluted by the limits of standard business assumptions and beliefs.

Current corporate sustainability efforts strive to make company practices less unsustainable. That's not good enough. To achieve sustainability, defined as 'the possibility that humans and other life will flourish on earth forever,' business (as well as other societal actors) must focus on practices that make the world more sustainable.

However, to make a positive impact on nature and resources rather than simply avoiding a negative impact, companies can't just do things better; they have to do things differently —

and that requires changing fundamental business mind-sets and assumptions about business operations, markets and competition.

To understand exactly how corporations must change their thinking, Haigh and Hoffman studied what they call 'hybrid' organizations — organizations that produce profits but that have sustainability missions at the heart of their reasons-for-being. One non-profit example of a hybrid organization is Kiva, an organization that provides microfinancing for entrepreneurs in the developing world. A for-profit example is Eden Foods, a natural food company that works to advance sustainable farming practices and food processing techniques.

Based on a comprehensive review of the research into hybrid organizations, also known as fourth sector or social enterprises, Haigh and Hoffman developed four propositions that describe how the hybrid organizations challenge standard business beliefs, a fifth proposition that explains their rationale for launching these challenges, and a sixth proposition that covers the way in which they enact sustainability.

These six propositions are as follows:

Proposition 1: Hybrid organizations decouple organizational success from the assumed need for perpetual economic growth. Hybrid organizations reject the notion that perpetual and infinite growth is required for economic success. Instead, they manage the pace of their growth so that they can focus as well on their social and environmental goals.

Proposition 2: Hybrid organizations adopt innovations that subordinate profit and create shared value. Sustainability does not need a 'business case' to prove its value. Creating shared value through initiatives that may hurt profits but improves sustainability is good enough.

Proposition 3: Hybrid organizations create shared value by cultivating close relationships with social and ecological systems in which they operate. Traditionally, companies adopt an internal-external dichotomy that places business-related issues as 'internal' issue while sustainability initiatives are viewed as helping 'external' stakeholders or systems. Hybrid organizations do not disassociate themselves from social and ecological systems.

Proposition 4: Hybrid organizations strive for an understanding of the intrinsic value of nature that goes beyond utility resource value. Finally, the traditional view of nature's value is as a resource to be used. For hybrid organizations, nature has intrinsic value beyond its role as a resource.

Proposition 5: Hybrid organizations challenge notions of control over resources, causal ambiguity, and market protection – and rather exemplify transparency of knowledge and information. Hybrid companies believe you can maintain a high level of transparency (e.g., open source technology) and still be competitive.

Proposition 6: Hybrid organizations simultaneously facilitate reducing negative environmental/societal impacts and increasing positive environmental/societal impacts. When enacting sustainable business models and practices, hybrid organizations don't only focus on becoming less unsustainable, but are especially focused on becoming more sustainable. The company Sun Oven produces solar cooking equipment, for example. At the core of its mission is the desire to improve the standard of living in developing countries, were unhealthy, indoor open-fire cooking is not uncommon.

BUSINESS APPLICATION

If as a corporate leader, you view sustainability as an 'external' issue, separate from your business imperatives, your company's journey toward social responsibility has just begun. You and your company may have taken significant steps to help society and the planet, but you can do more.

A first step: Do not be satisfied with only doing 'less harm.' How can your company make a positive impact on the environment and society?

Another important step is to change your perspective on nature as only a resource. While protecting resources is important, nature has more to offer your company than you might realize. For example, companies that use bio-mimicry, such as adopting the 'engineering' of the humpback whale fin to surfboards, fans, turbines or pumps, recognize the intrinsic value of nature beyond its resources.

The most important and most difficult step in achieving sustainable goals: Challenge the basic tenets of business success, from profit and growth assumptions to accepted competitive advantage and value chain imperatives. Rejecting the basic rules of business may seem both self-destructive and impossible. The fundamental lesson of this research is that challenging the dogma of business can be done: just ask the fearless heretics known as hybrid companies.

REFERENCES
The New Heretics: Hybrid Organizations and the Challenges They Present to Corporate Sustainability. Nardia Haigh & Andrew J. Hoffman. Organization & Environment (September 2014).

Access this and more Ideas at **ideasforleaders.com**

Book Reviews

Robot Souls

Programming in
Humanity

By Eve Poole

*Published by CRC Press (Taylor
& Francis) – August 2023, 184
pages, ISBN: 978-1032426624*

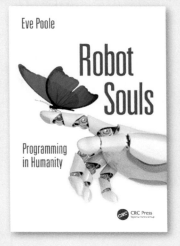

The extraordinary pace of progress of Artificial Intelligence (AI) in recent years, most notably with the ability of us all to access it through the likes of ChatGPT and Google Bard, has put pressure on everyone to understand the threats and opportunities that it presents for us as individuals, as organizations and existentially.

Loose fears of AI presenting us with an existential crisis abound, though it is much more difficult to get anyone to actually present a realistic scenario of how this might occur. There is very little 'loose' however in this book. The author embraces the topic of managing

AI in a bravura display of knowledge and concision. This book covers a startling breadth of topics in under 150 pages, including some 40 pages of notes and references.

Poole is an accomplished academic as well as educator and former Commissioner of the Church of England – all roles that play informative parts in this exploration of AI and the soul.

While the title of the book suggests a single enquiry into how we might adapt and evolve AI to behave in a way that is conscientious and self-aware, the foundations for such an exploration require an examination of what is AI, what makes us human and why that is important, and what is the Soul. To do this Poole takes us on a journey through philosophy from the ancients to present-day, global culture, religion, literature, neuroscience and commerce. It is a fascinating and enlightening journey.

The key waymarks are: Iain McGilchrist's stance on the West's over-emphasis on data-based left-brain analysis, at the expense of the synthesizing qualities of right-brain perceptions; Moravec's Paradox, that it is relatively easy to train machines to do things we find difficult (like maths and logic) but difficult to get them to do the things we don't even think about (like walking, moving, image recognition); and John Searle's Chinese Room thought-experiment, which highlights the difference between providing an answer and understanding it.

Poole agrees with McGilchrist's view that we have become overly focused on STEM-based certainty at the expense of humanities-based uncertainty. In a world that has been preaching the existence of VUCA for the last three decades this is peculiar, but in terms of computing no doubt broadly correct. Her particular insight that ties the human brain to the coded one, is that in coding developers write 'junk code' that is either redundant or irrelevant, and that for humans we also have code that if appraised by a developer may be classed as junk code, that is it gets in the way of a clean, objective output.

Poole breaks human junk code down into seven elements: emotions, mistakes, story-telling, sixth sense, uncertainty, free will and meaning. None of these elements improves the efficiency of transactions but all are integral to making life richer. They are elements that make us human. Having identified them, we also see that they are fundamental to society, that is without them we would be hugely challenged to build community, and without community we lose the 'human magic' that keeps us at the top of the animal hierarchy.

Thus far, I think the author brilliantly dissects what Bagehot might describe as the efficient and the dignified sides of humanity. When bringing it to AI she suggests that we build-in these seven junk code elements so that AI can acquire these sensibilities too. Something about this jars however, it is both a 'playing God' solution, she says "if God made us in his image...we should extend that favour to these new creations that we are making in our image" ... "we should be able to prime our AI with as full a range of philosophies of life as we can muster, and give it the capacity to parse them in context"; and there will remain an absence of authenticity about it, we will know that it is only simulated.

Nonetheless, the author takes this polemic out into the open, and provides us with important tools and ideas to further it with. Time remains of the essence, but we will all benefit from understanding this topic better, and Poole's extended essay is a hugely valuable, entertaining, and informative step forward.

Talking Heads

The New Science of How Conversation Shapes Our Worlds

By Shane O'Mara

Published: August 2023, ISBN: 978-1847926487

S hane O'Mara is the possessor of the most enviable job title, Professor of Experimental Brain Research, at Trinity College Dublin, and by his own description explores how 'the brain meets the world'. This very engaging book, filled with accessible explanations and real-world impact, is perhaps best explained the other way around however – how the world has been shaped by our brains.

The title itself is something of a red herring, the focus of the book is less about conversation – at least the kinds of conversation we engage in on a daily basis – and more about memory and how we individually and collectively recall the things we experience and the things we learn and interpret, and how we shape the world around us according to those recollections.

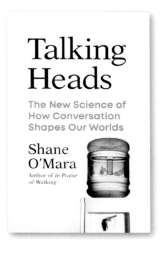

O'Mara's central point is that the geo-political world we have created is very largely a function of how our memory, both individual and collective, has presented these facts to us. He is less forth-coming, though touches on, how our memories are coloured by our emotions – and how our emotions are instrumental in shaping the conversations we have that lead to the actions that enable us to build the nation states we have created.

As a neuroscientist, the book is founded on the brain activity that occurs to enable our memories. The majority of research that is done on this, is with those who have had brain damage and as a result lost memory function.

The book opens with the case of Henry Molaison, who as a boy in the 1930s had a bicycle accident which led to epilepsy; to cure this he underwent an experimental operation in his late 20s to remove a part of his brain. The operation brought immediate relief to his fits, but his memory of anything subsequent to the operation, beyond very recent moments, was completely lost. This did not affect his IQ/reasoning function or his ability to focus – but he was unable to recall any context for any situation. Everyone was constantly new to him too.

This case highlights how critical our ability to remember is to support our ability to create change. As O'Mara says 'we depend on memory, all of the time, to make our complex, social lives possible.' Our 'memories are a multi-layered record, subtly over-written and updated on the fly as we converse within our social groups'.

The ability to both remember and to present our remembered thoughts and ideas are critical for such social animals as humans. O'Mara also notes that humans occupy a sweetspot on the social spectrum that allows us to live in very large groups. Comparing us to our closest primates – if we were more solitary like orang-utans there would be less communication, and if we were more given to violence like chimpanzees our ability to live in city-sized groups would be *much impaired*.

But we do occupy this spot, and so social interaction is extensive. To do so effectively requires certain skills to optimize conversations though. He notes the gap between one person stopping speaking and the other

Humans 'crave the connections and shared understanding that comes from sharing stories..., but the story always needs an emotional hook to it.

starting is typically around 200 milliseconds, as fast as is humanly possible; the inference being we have already formulated our response before the other has stopped speaking, anticipating what they will say. Most often this works well, but O'Mara notes, 'to change minds, you must talk with respect and listen with care...'.

It is really the stories we tell that shape the future. Humans 'crave the connections and shared understanding that comes from sharing stories..., but the story always needs an emotional hook to it. He also notes we have 'an in-bult propensity to share what we know with others', and later acknowledges 'we talk about ourselves to influence others'.

These are the roots of collective culture, and how groups and organizations create shared understandings; it also explains why we sometimes allow ourselves to 'go along to get along' so we can remain part of the in-group.

Memory underpins all of this. It is not just a way for us to picture the past, it allows us shortcuts to understand the present and foresee imagined futures. And this is why O'Mara sees it as playing such a critical role in the creation of modern nations.

About the Publishers

Ideas for Leaders

Ideas for Leaders summarizes the thinking of
the foremost researchers and experts on leadership and management
practice from the world's top business schools and management
research institutions. With these concise and easily readable 'Ideas'
you can quickly and easily inform yourself and your colleagues about
the latest insights into management best practice.

The research-based Ideas are supported by a growing series of
podcasts with influential thinkers, CEOs, and other leading leadership
and management experts from large organizations and small. We also
publish book reviews and a new series of online programs.

www.ideasforleaders.com

The Center for the Future of Organization (CFFO)

CFFO is an independent Think Tank and Research Center at the
Drucker School of Management at Claremont Graduate University.
The Center's mission is to deepen our understanding of new
capabilities that are critical to succeed in a digitally connected world,
and to support leaders and organizations along their transformational
journey.

In the tradition of Peter Drucker, the Center works across disciplines,
combining conceptual depth with practical applicability and ethical
responsibility, in close collaboration and connection with thought
leaders and practice leaders from academia, business, and consulting.

www.futureorg.org

PLANET EARTH FIRST

Please Take
Nothing But
Pictures
Leave Nothing
But Footprints

DLG Advisory Board

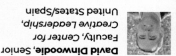

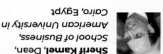